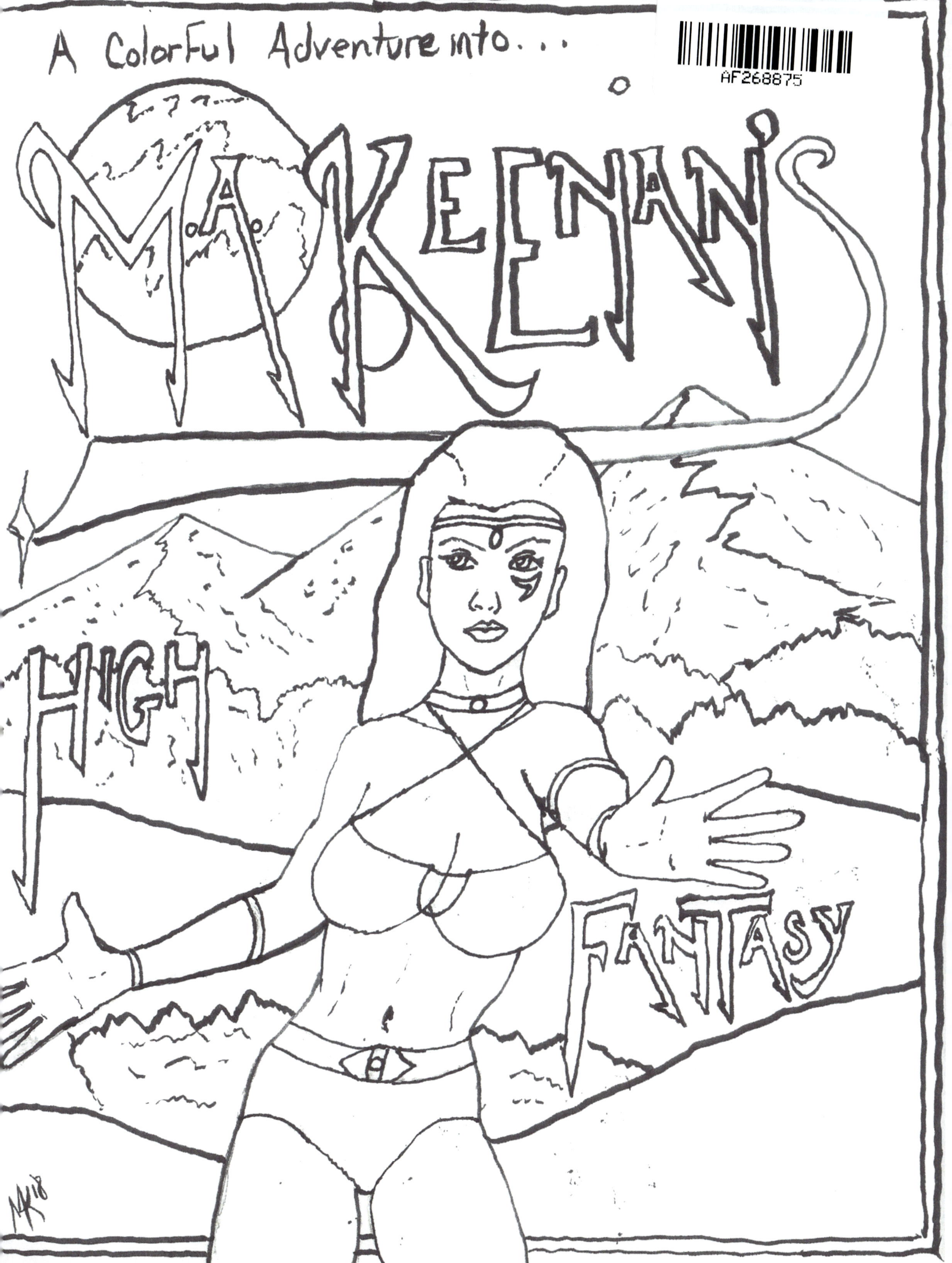

A Colorful Adventure into...
MaKEENAN'S
HIGH
FANTASY
AF268875

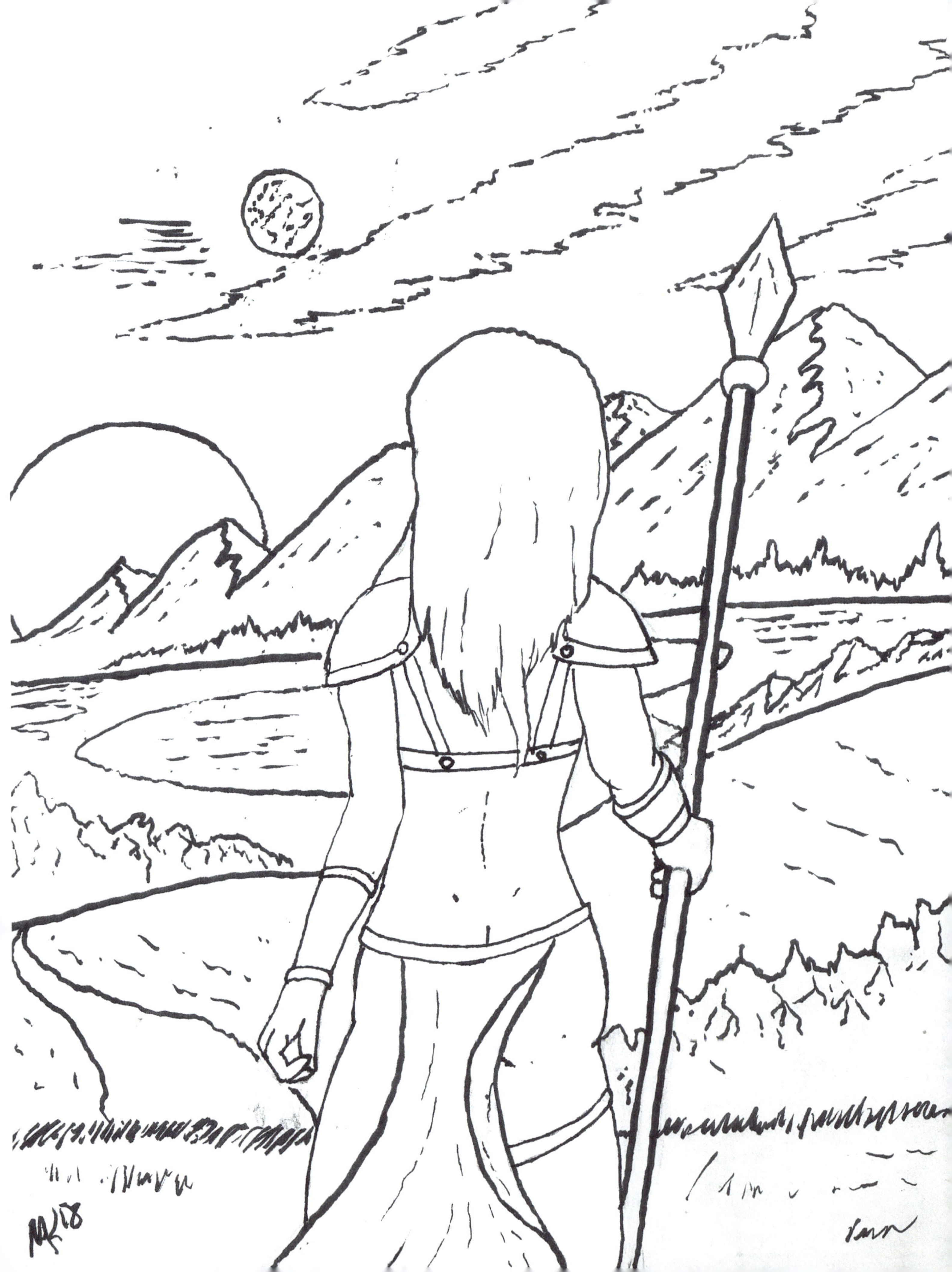

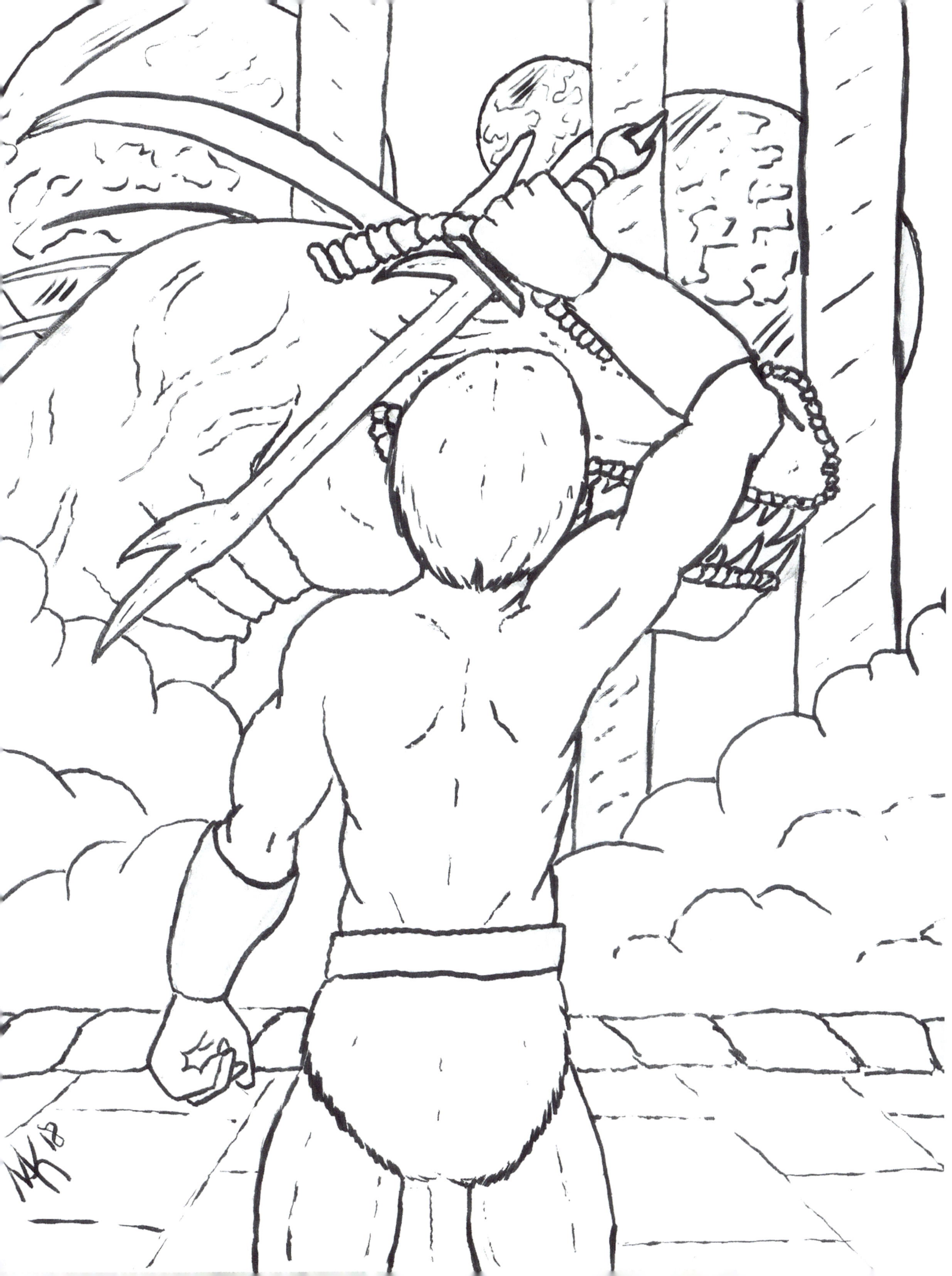

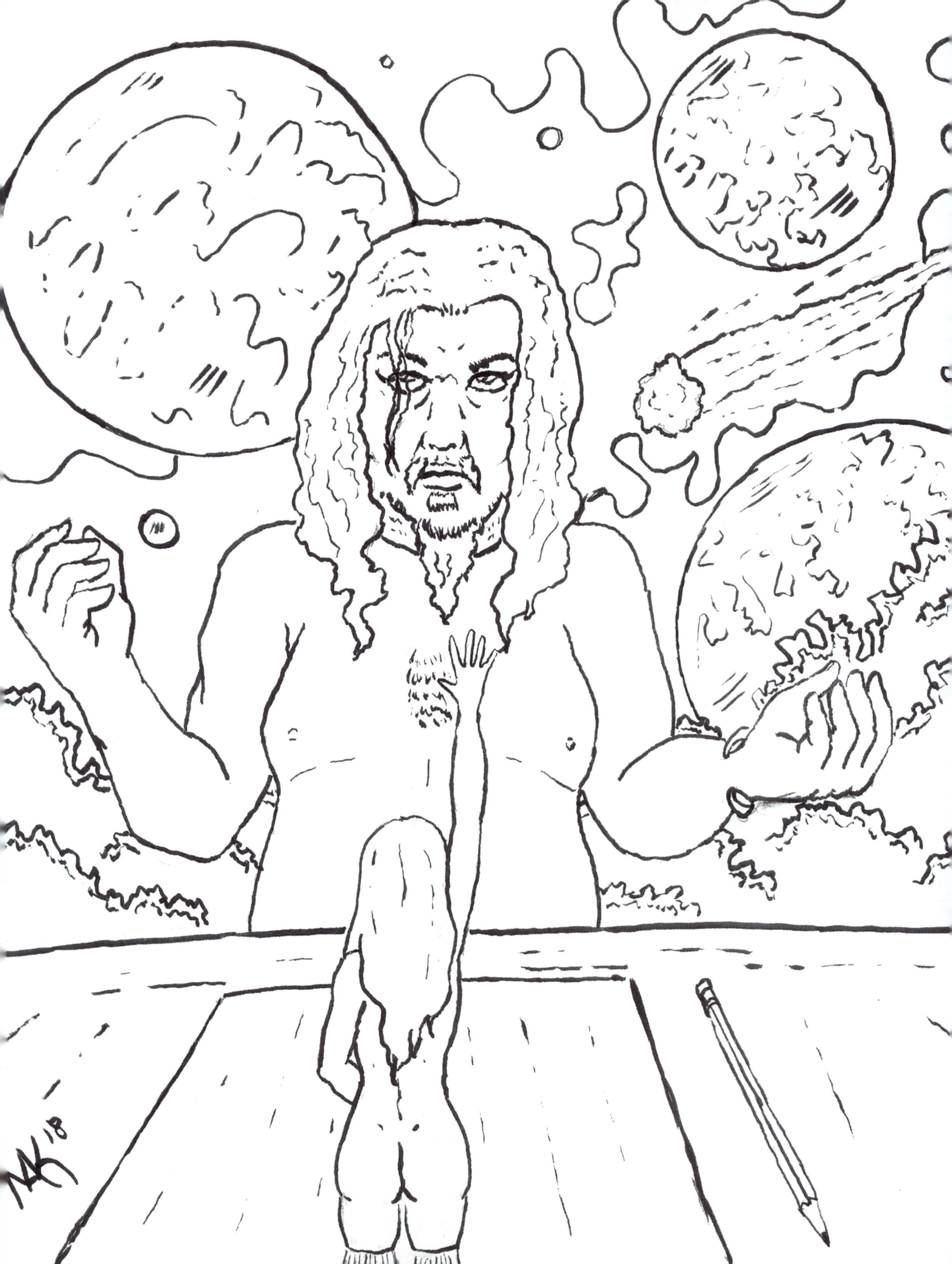

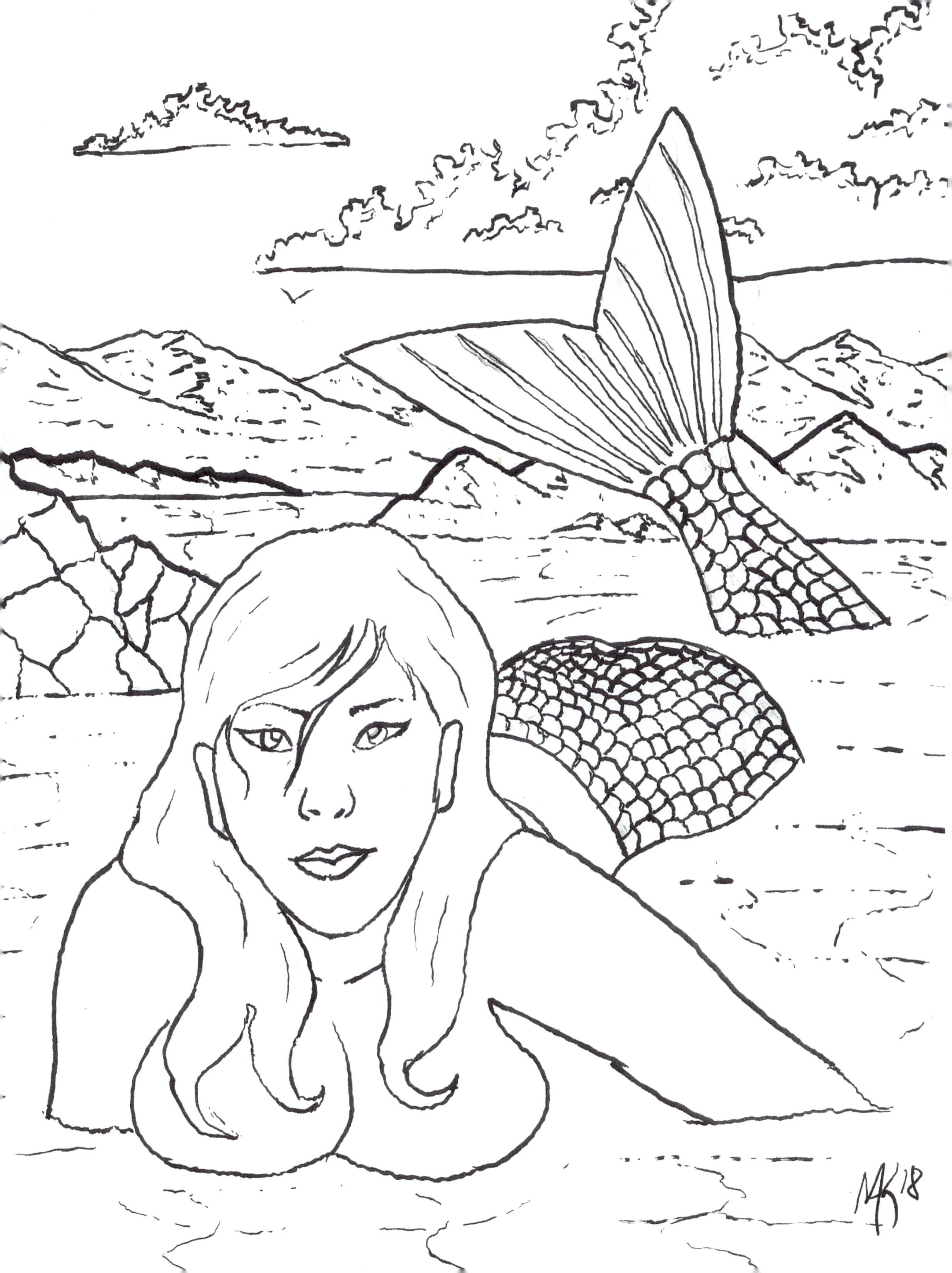

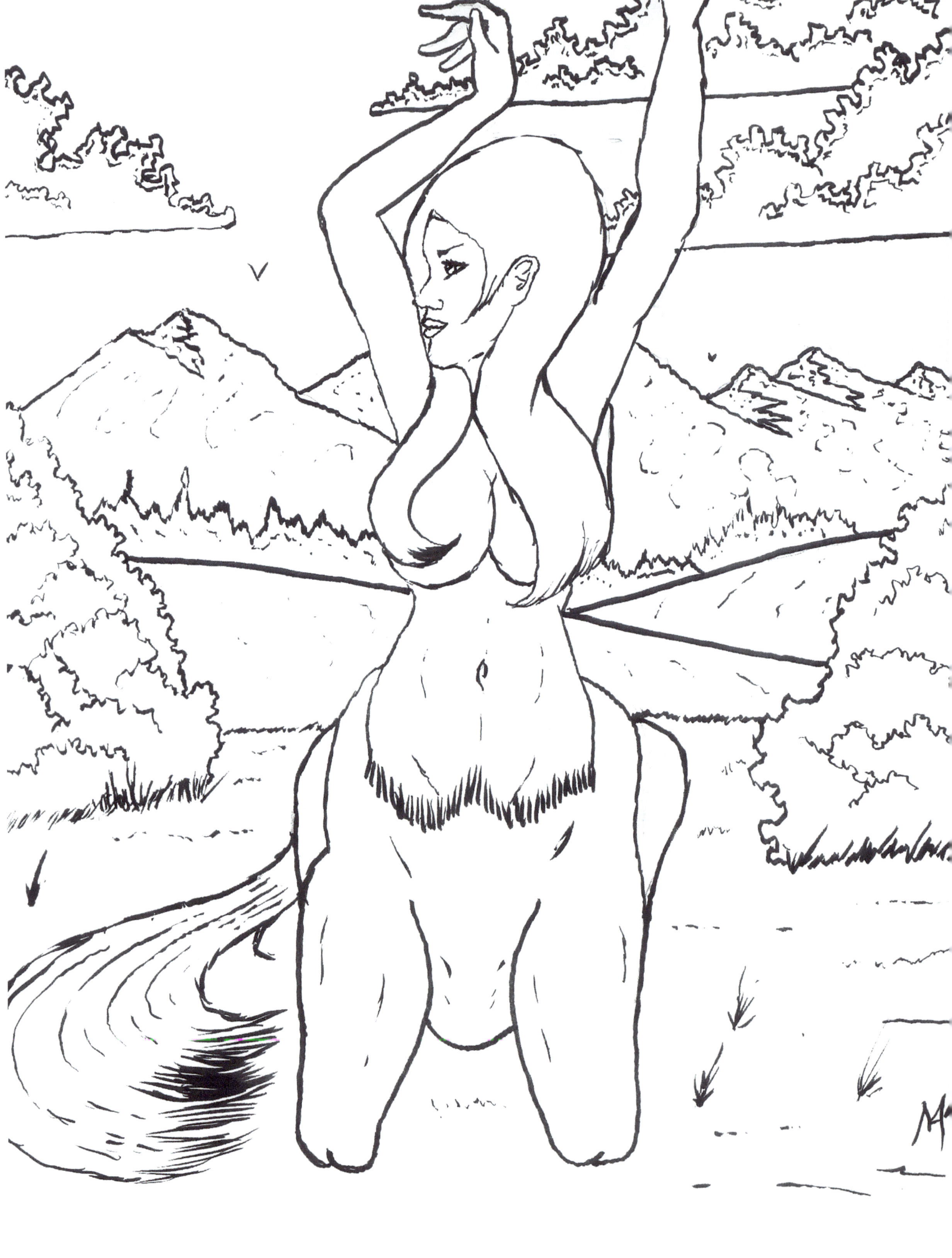

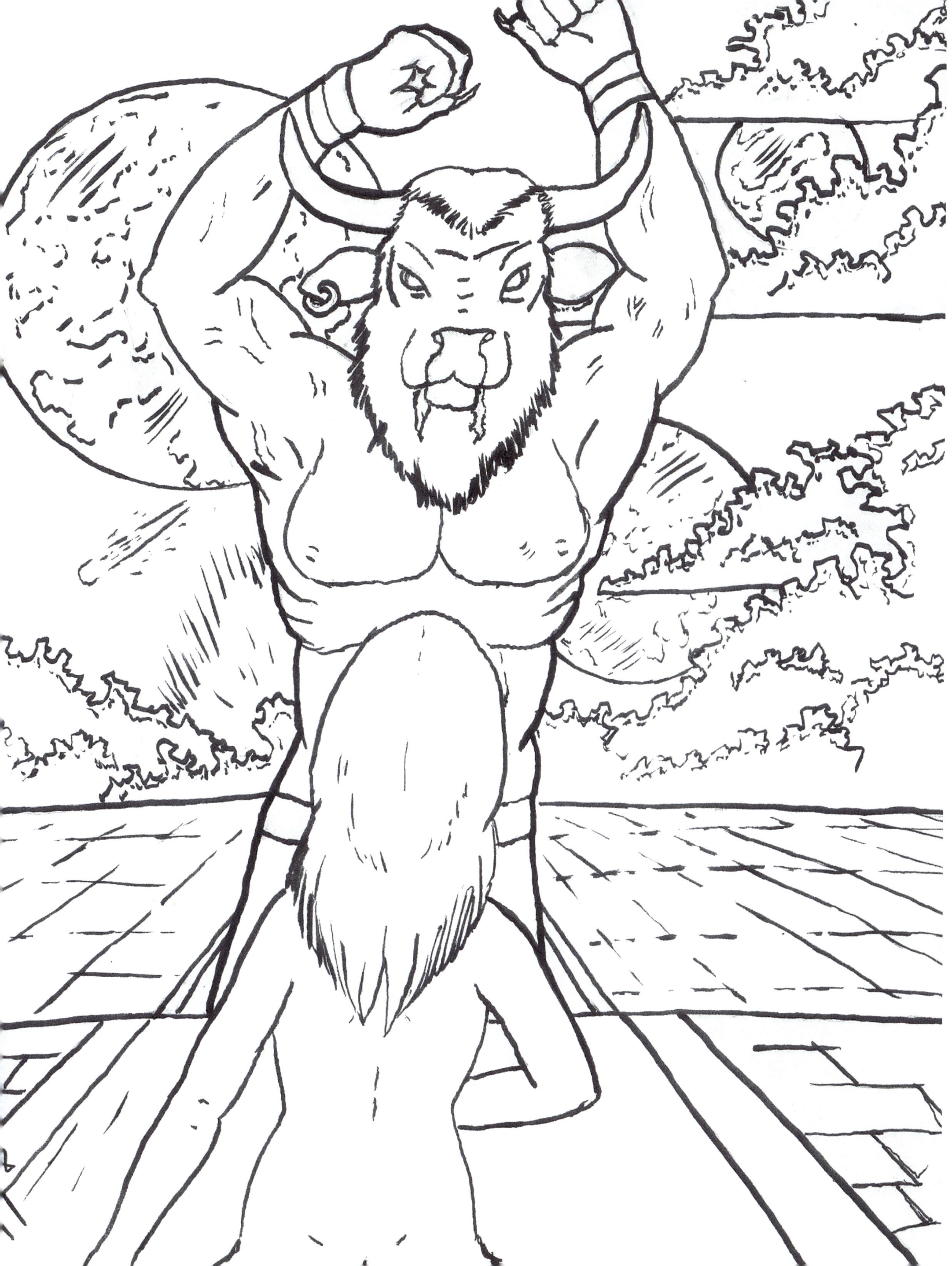

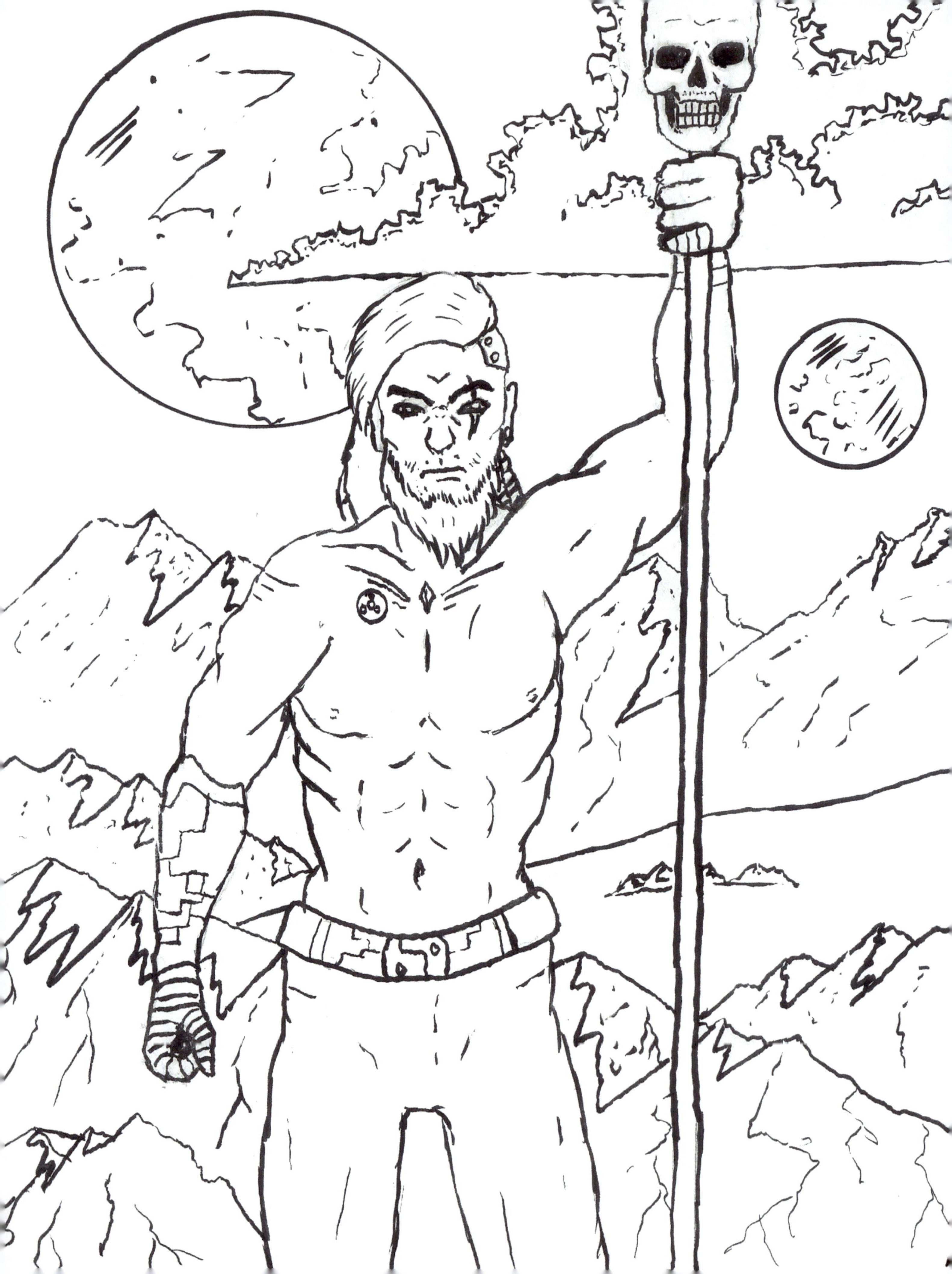

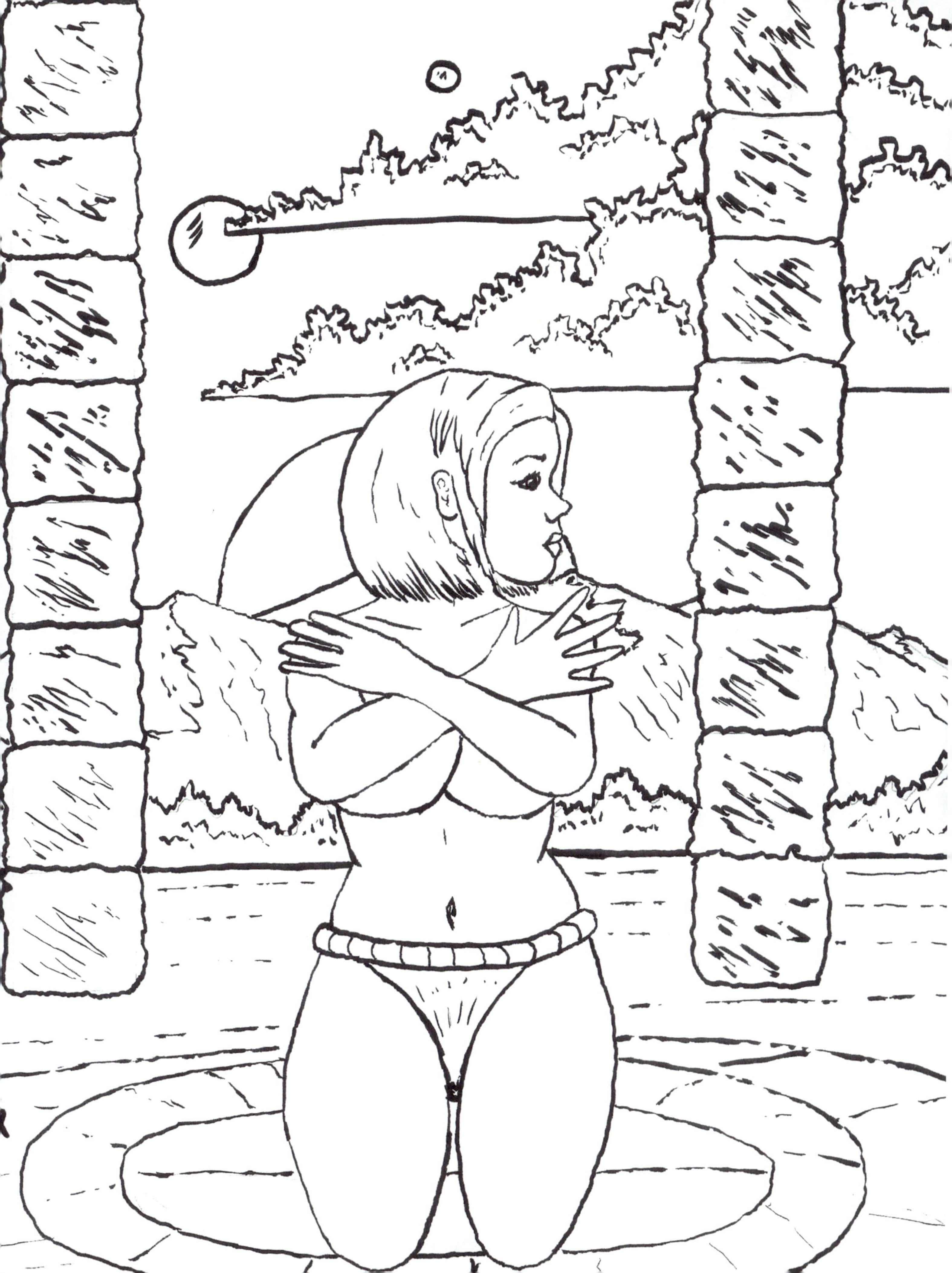

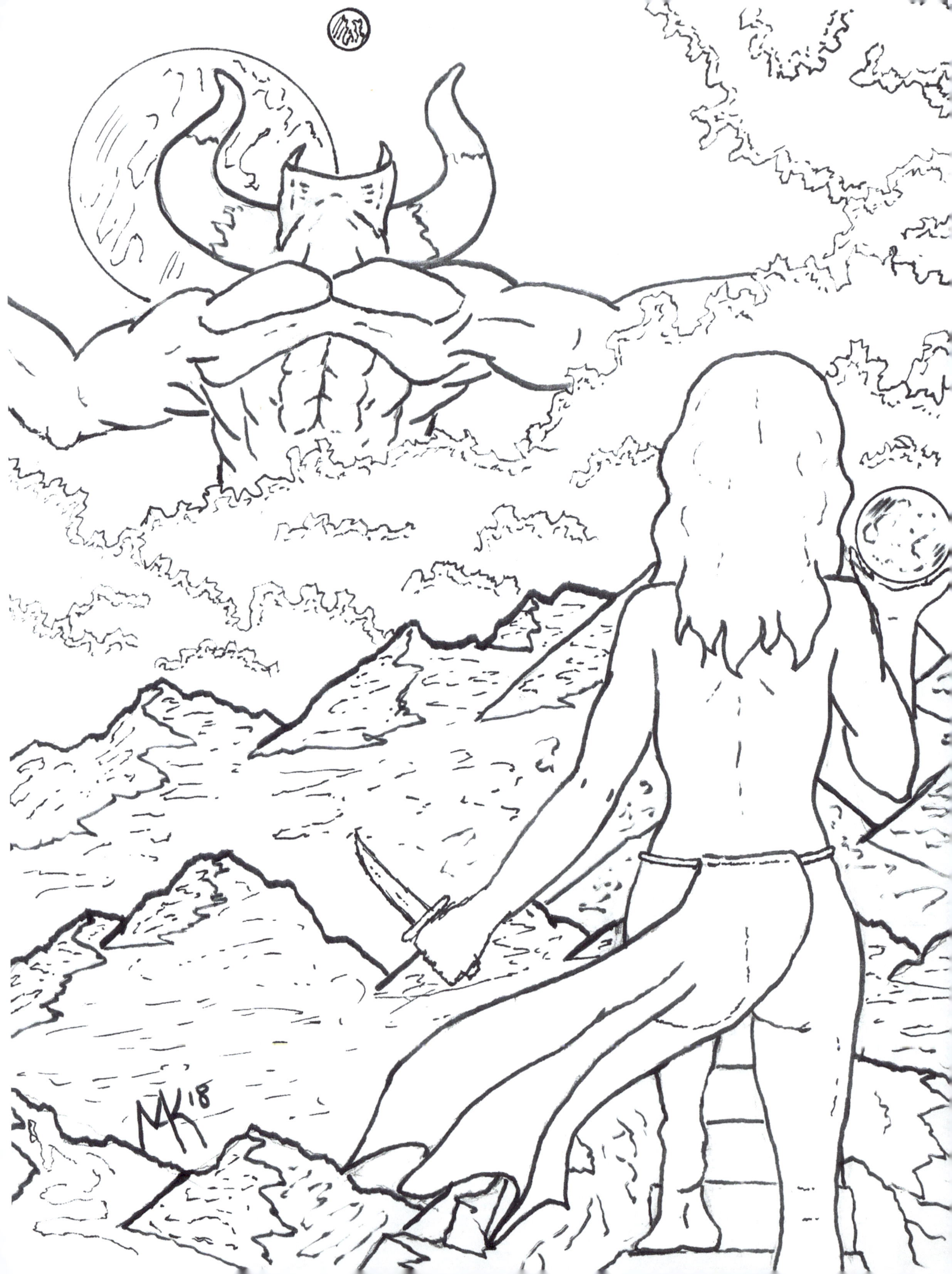

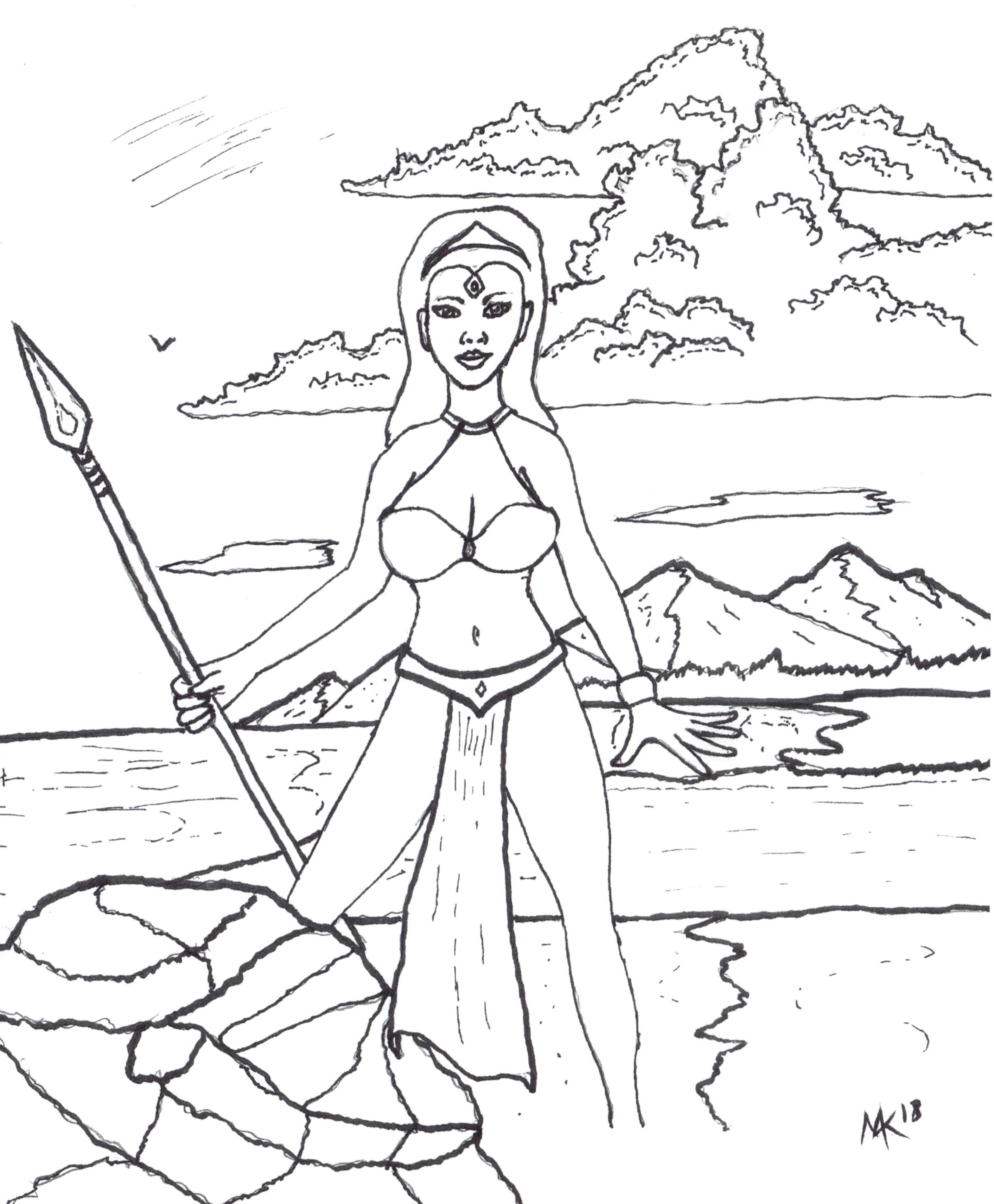

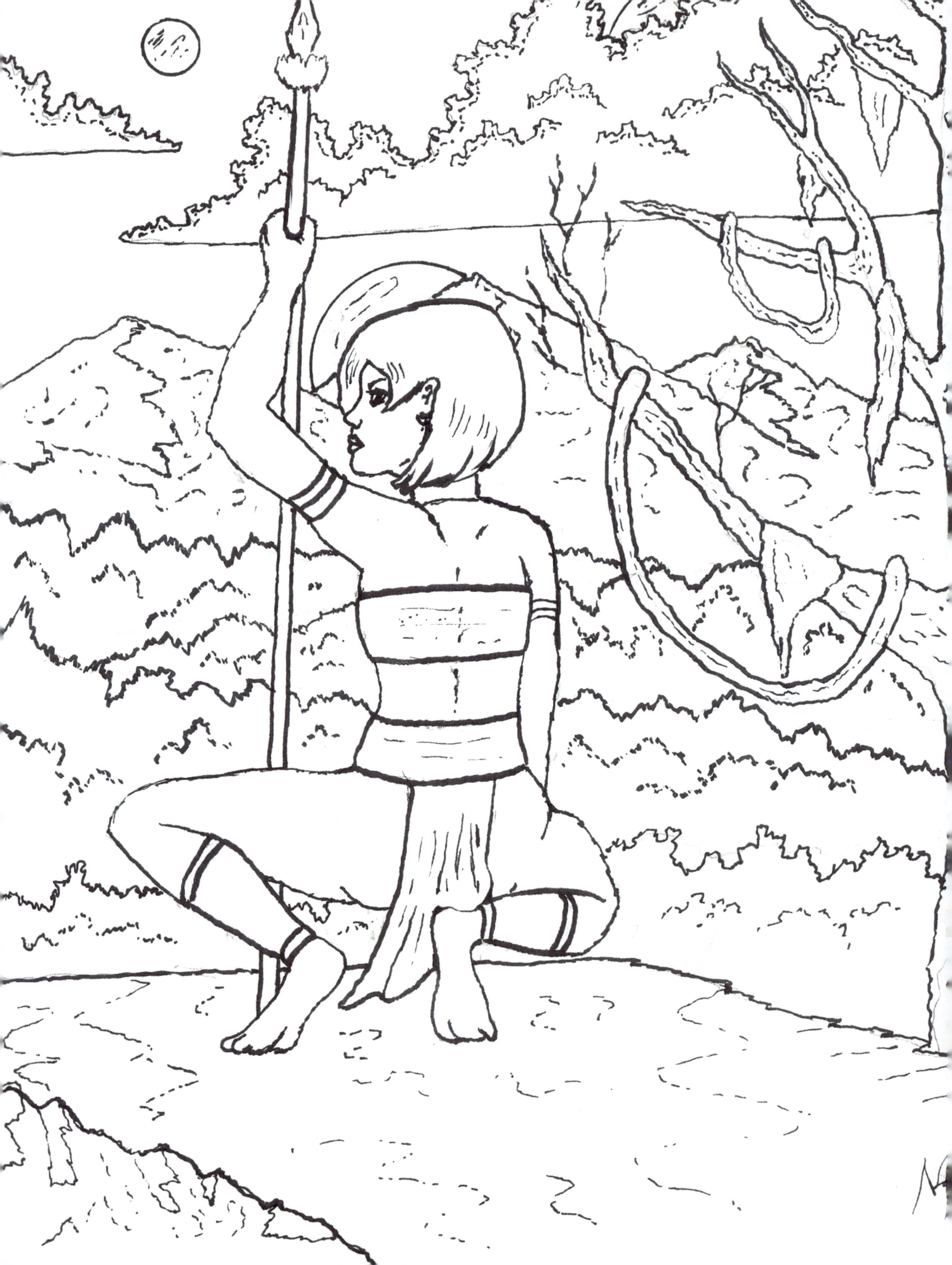

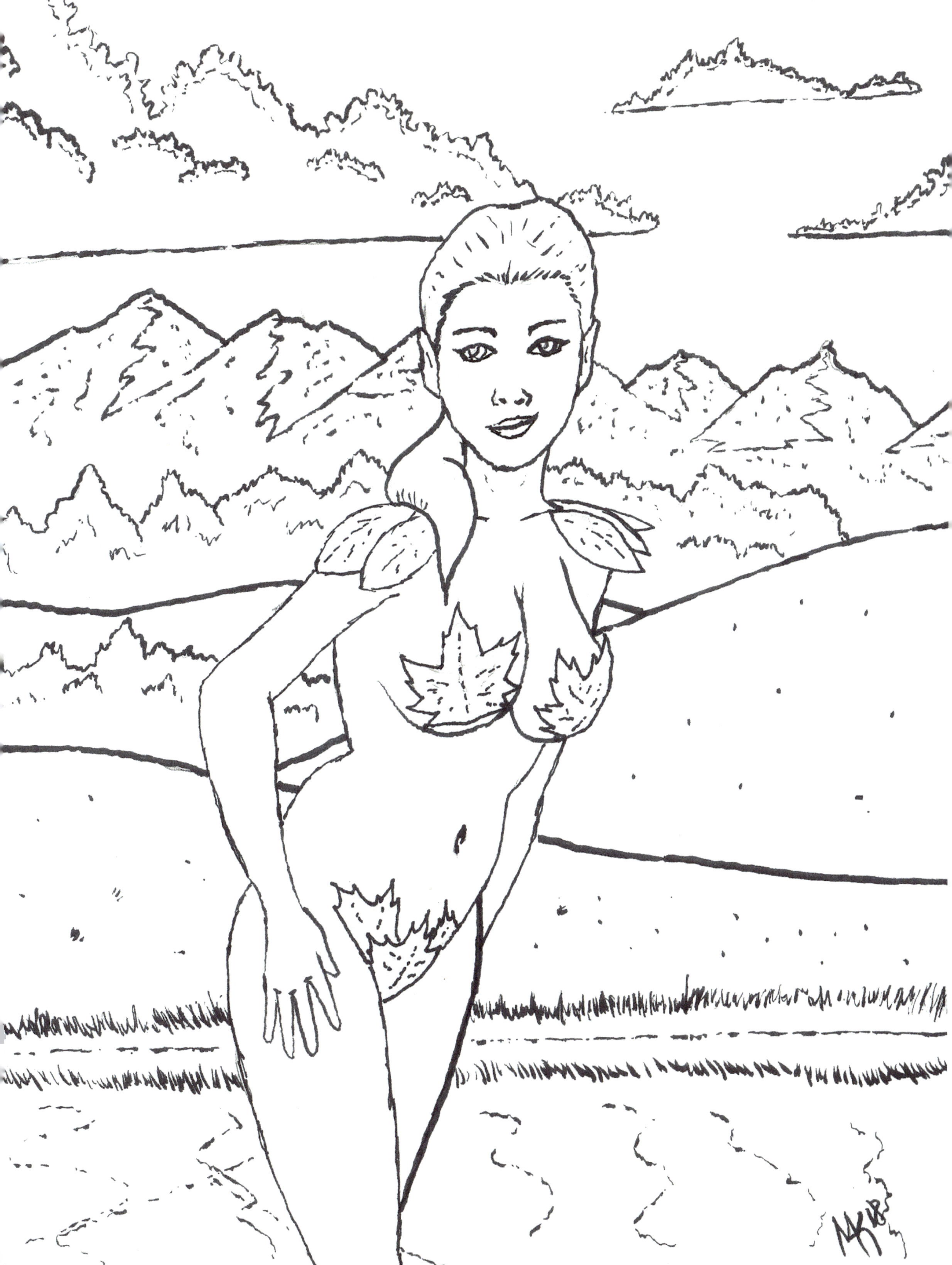

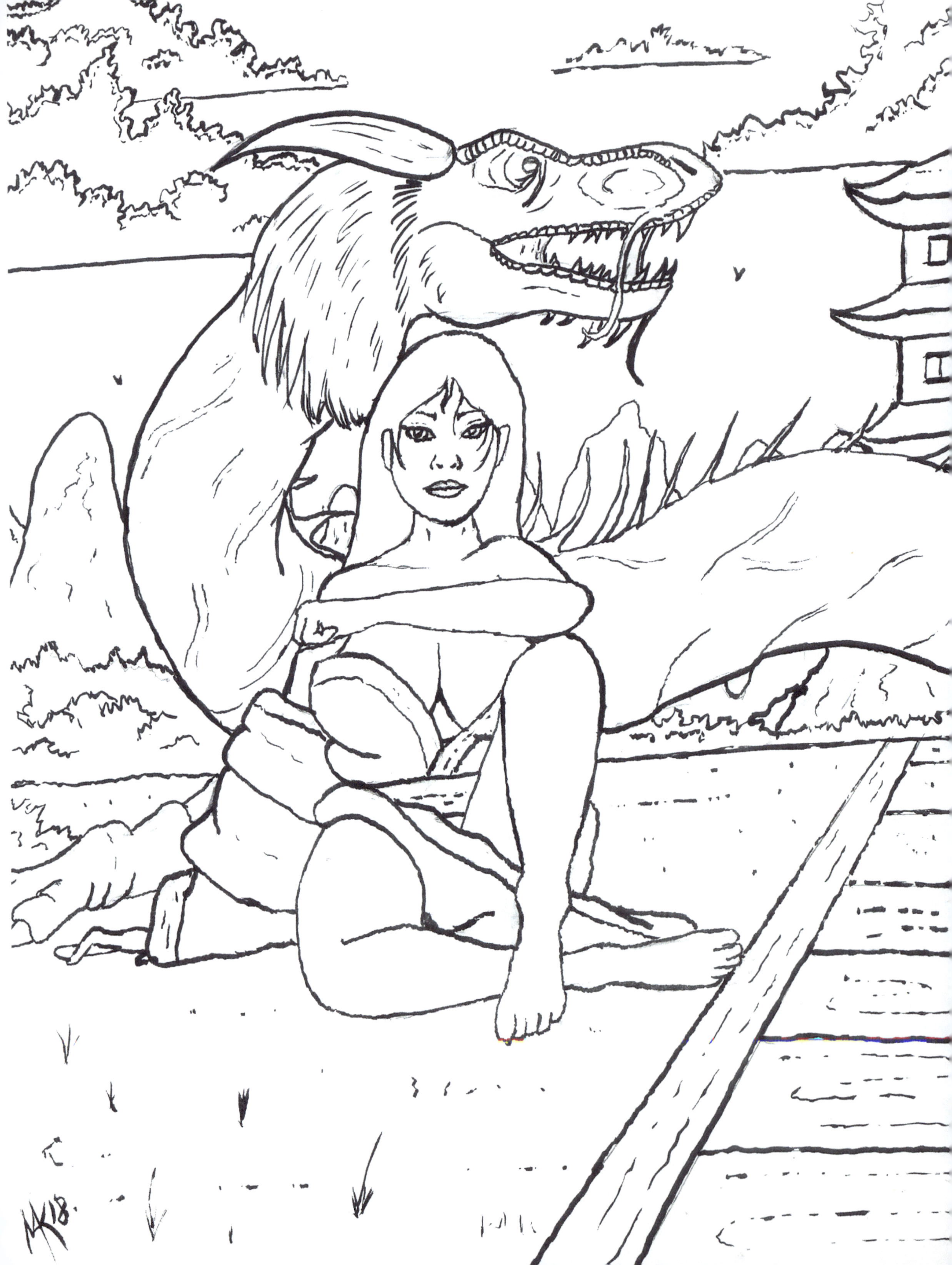

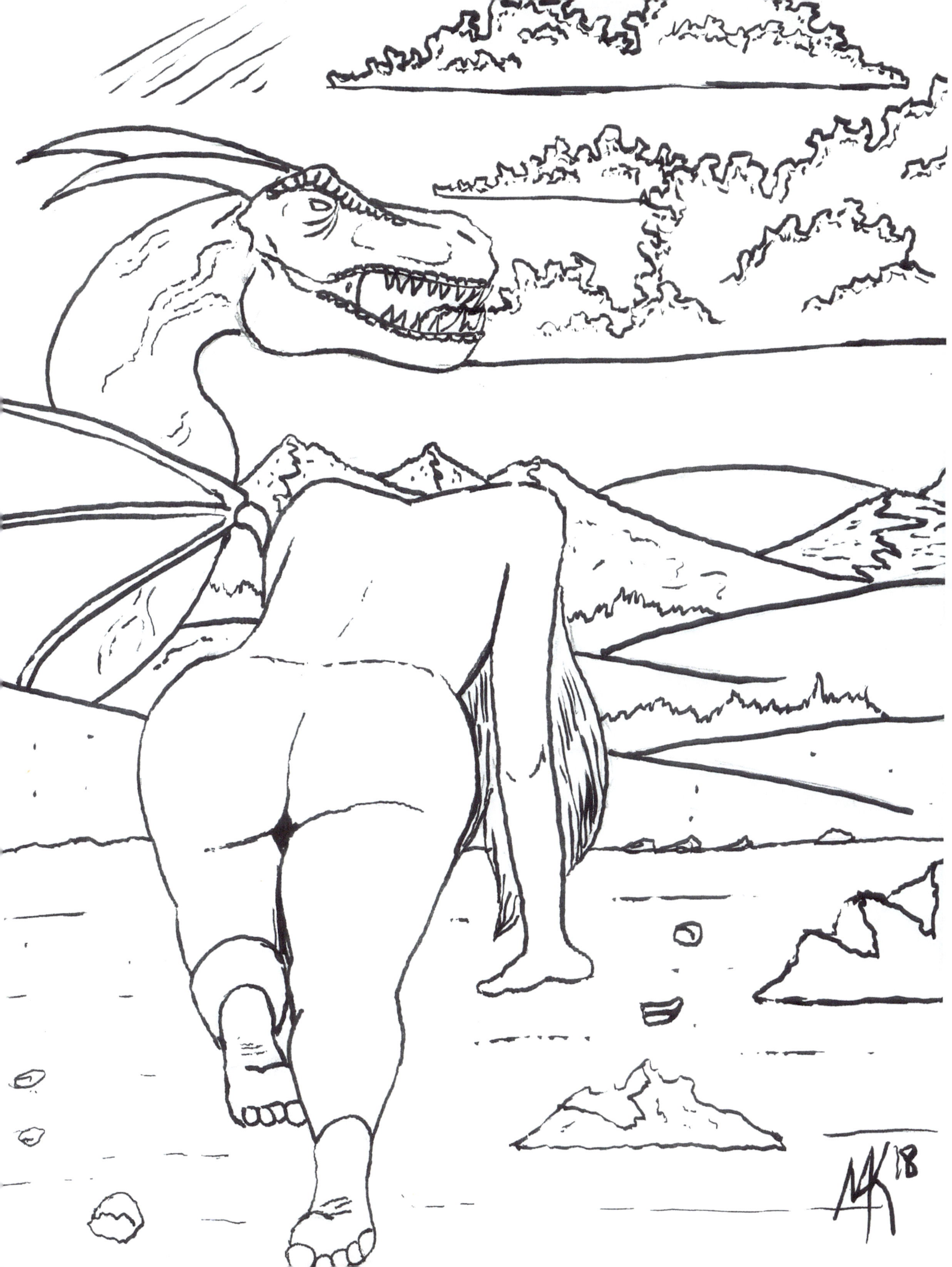

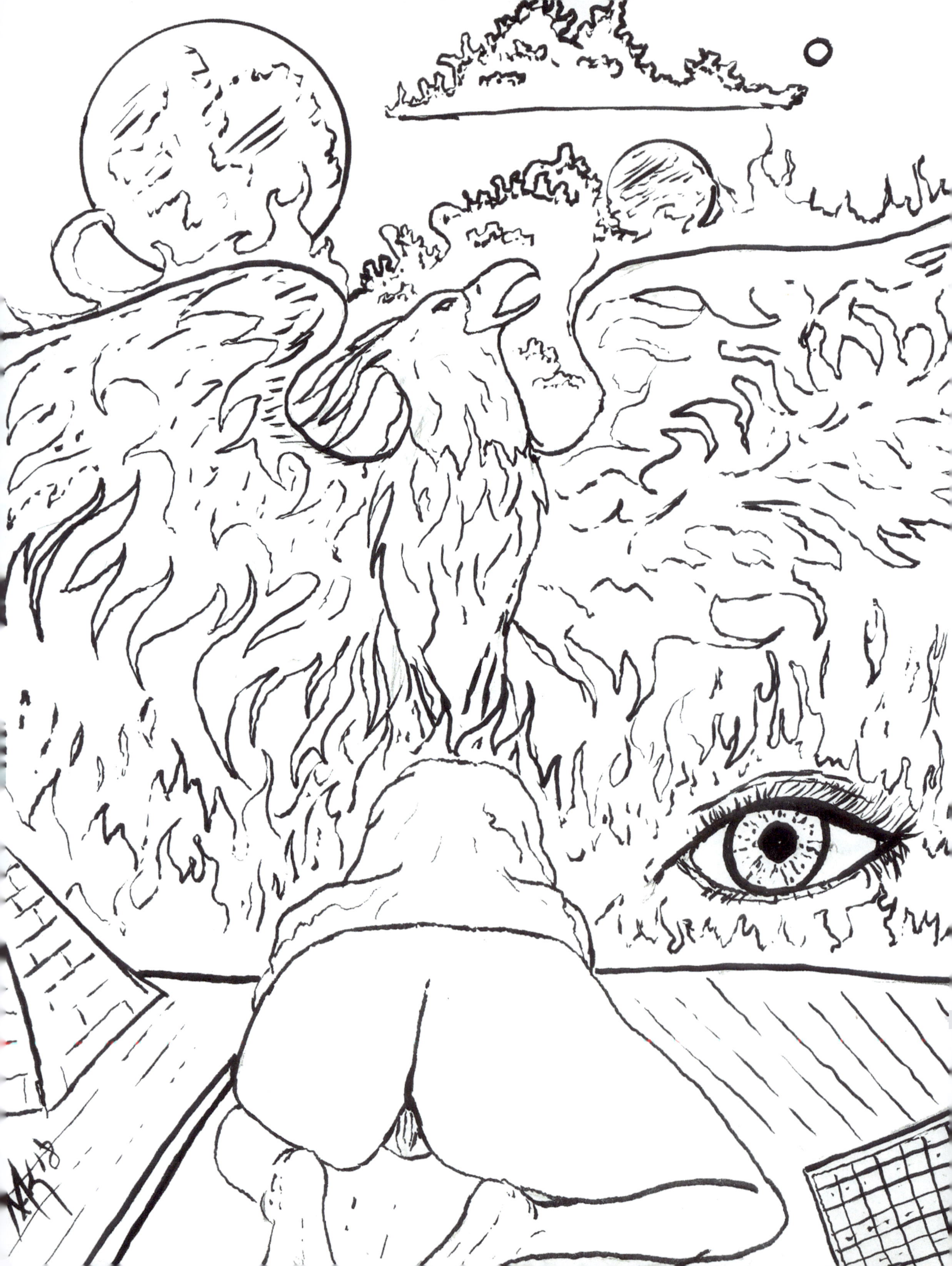

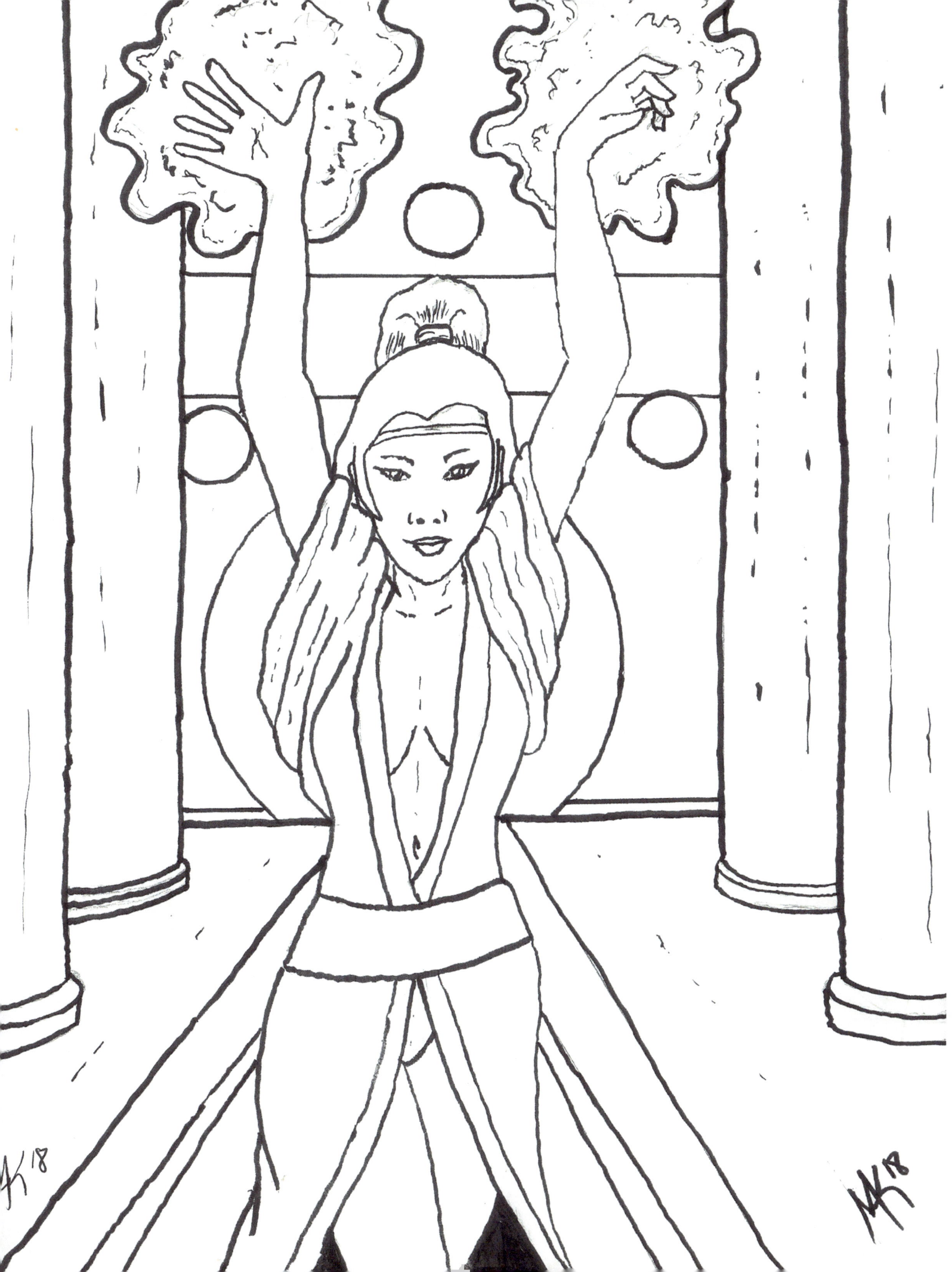

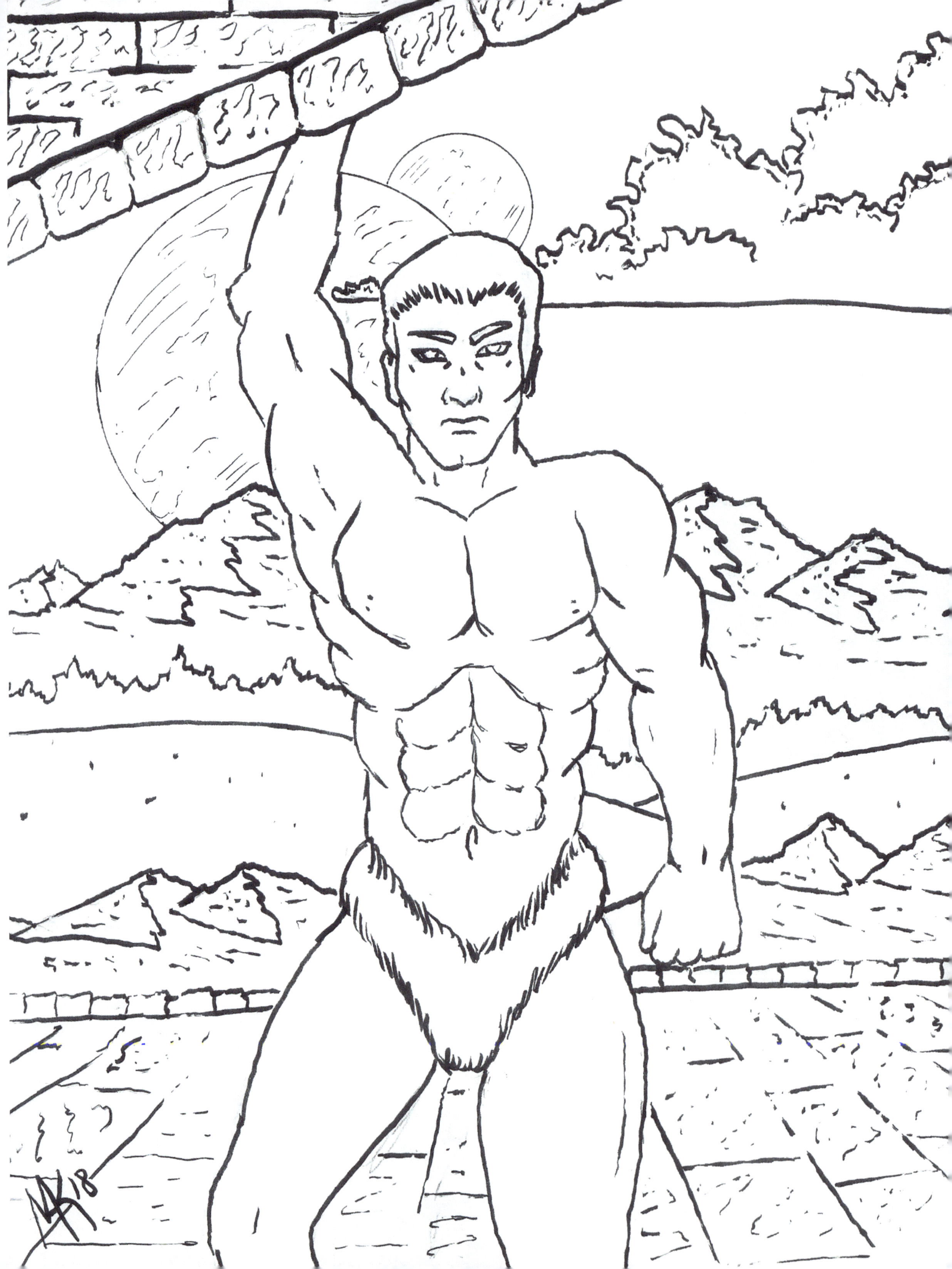

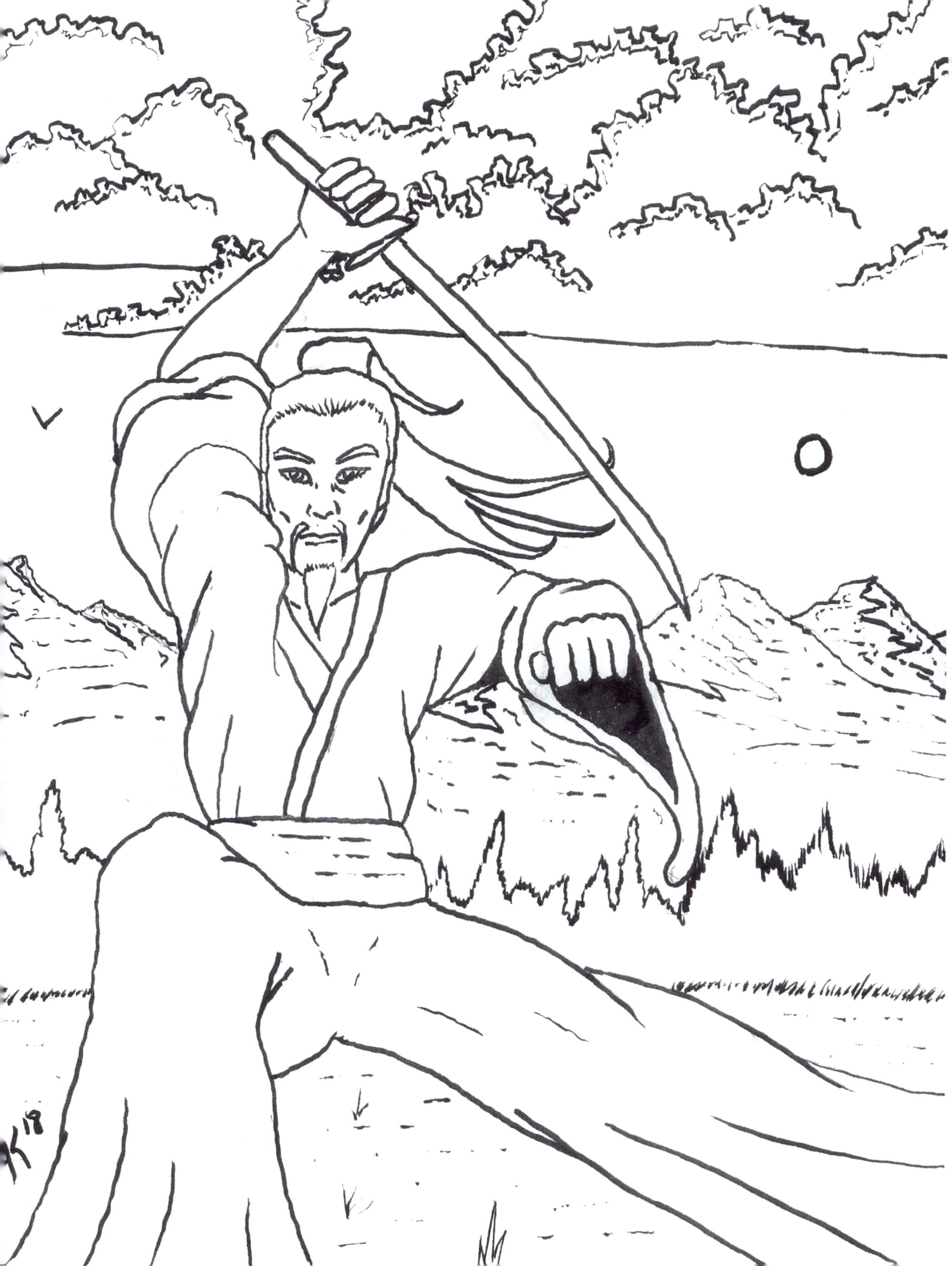

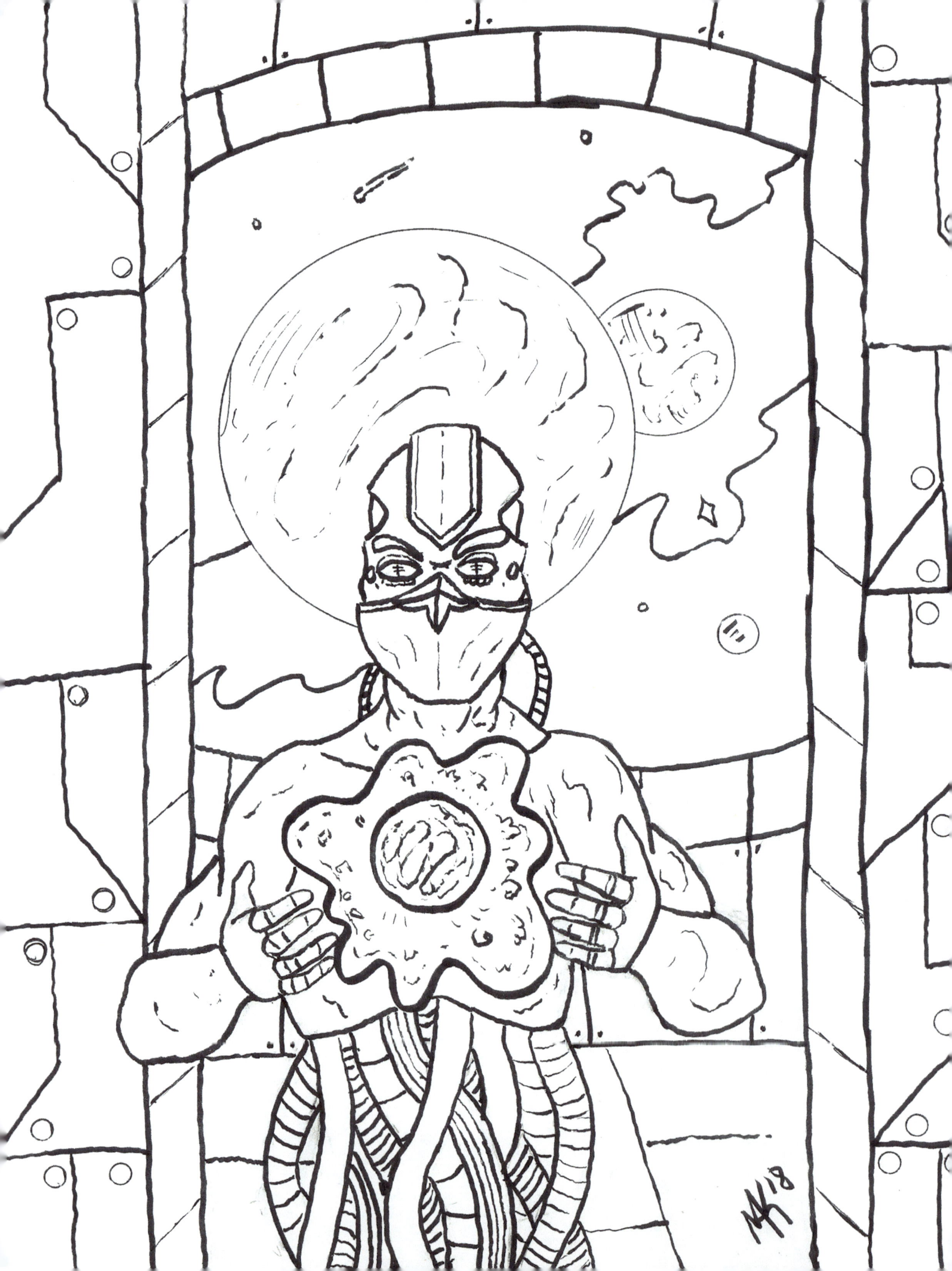

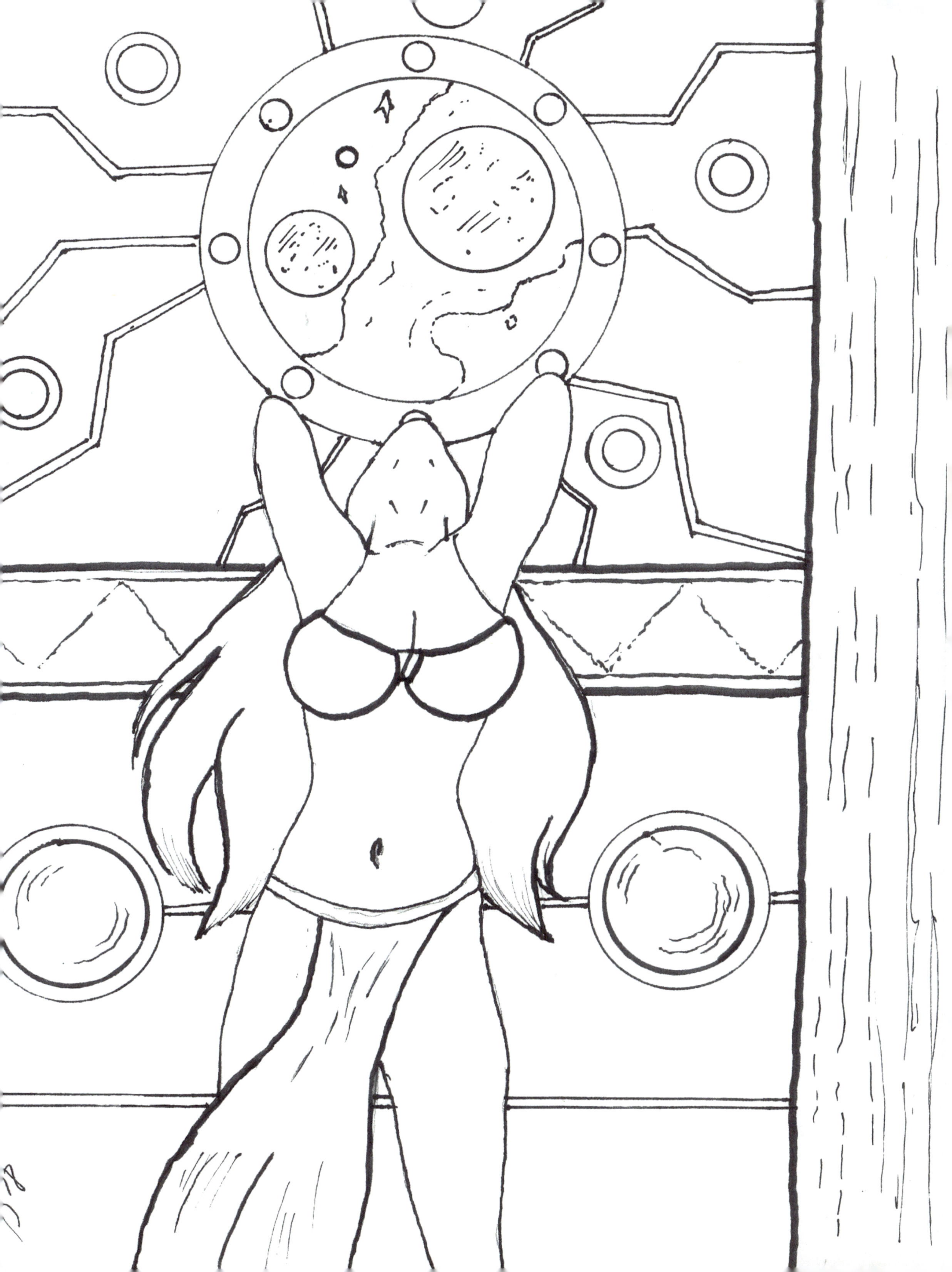

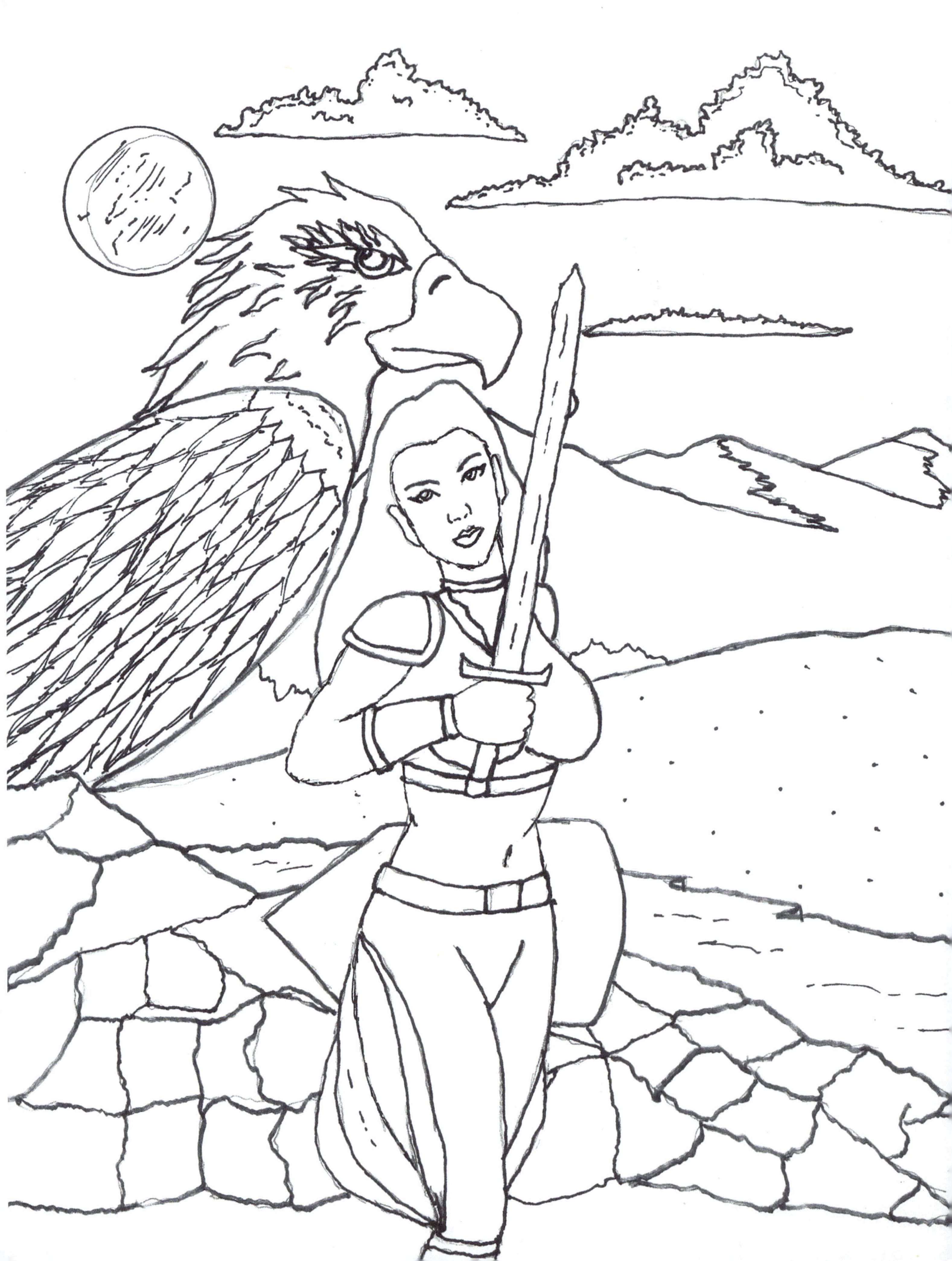

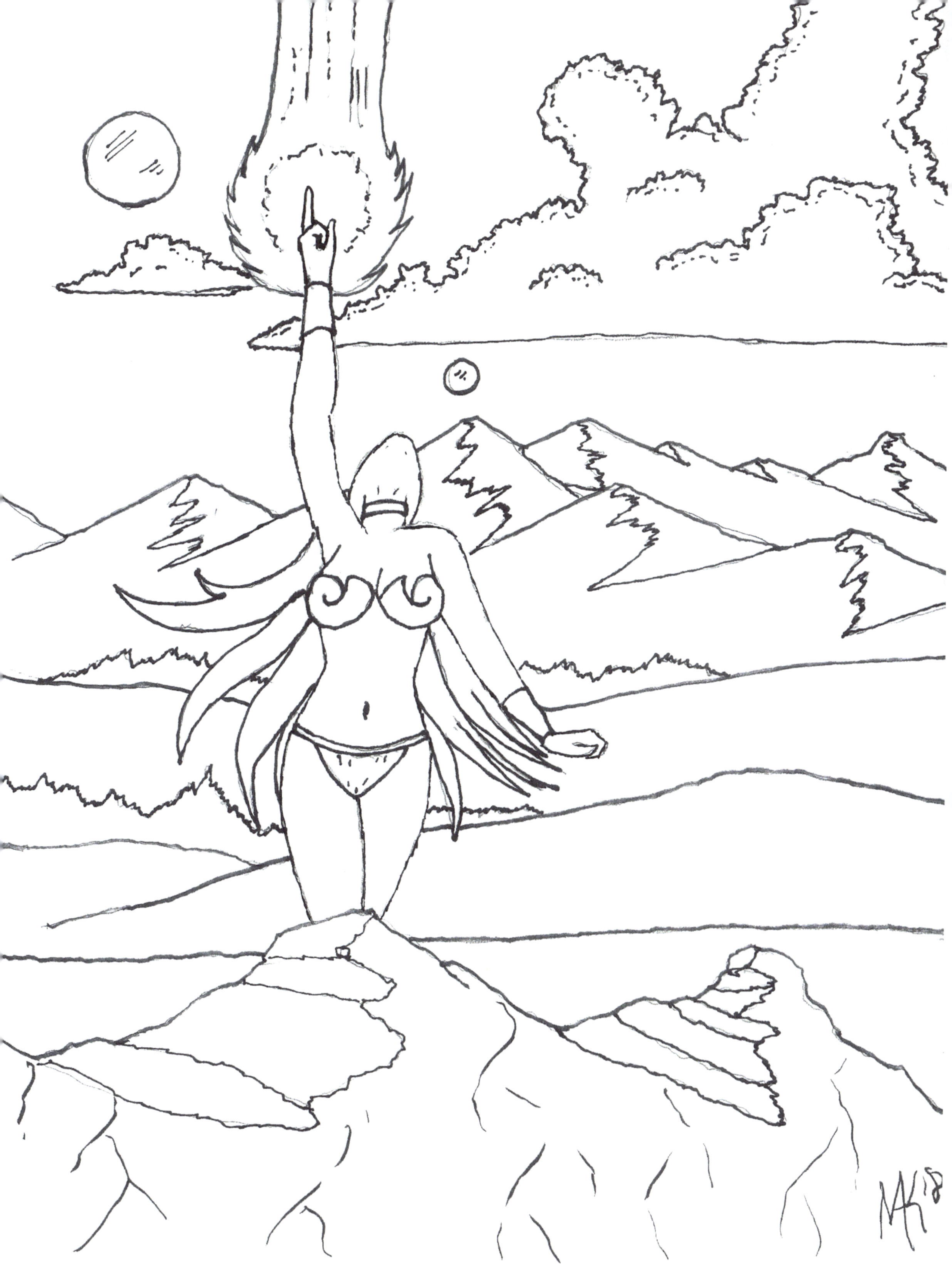

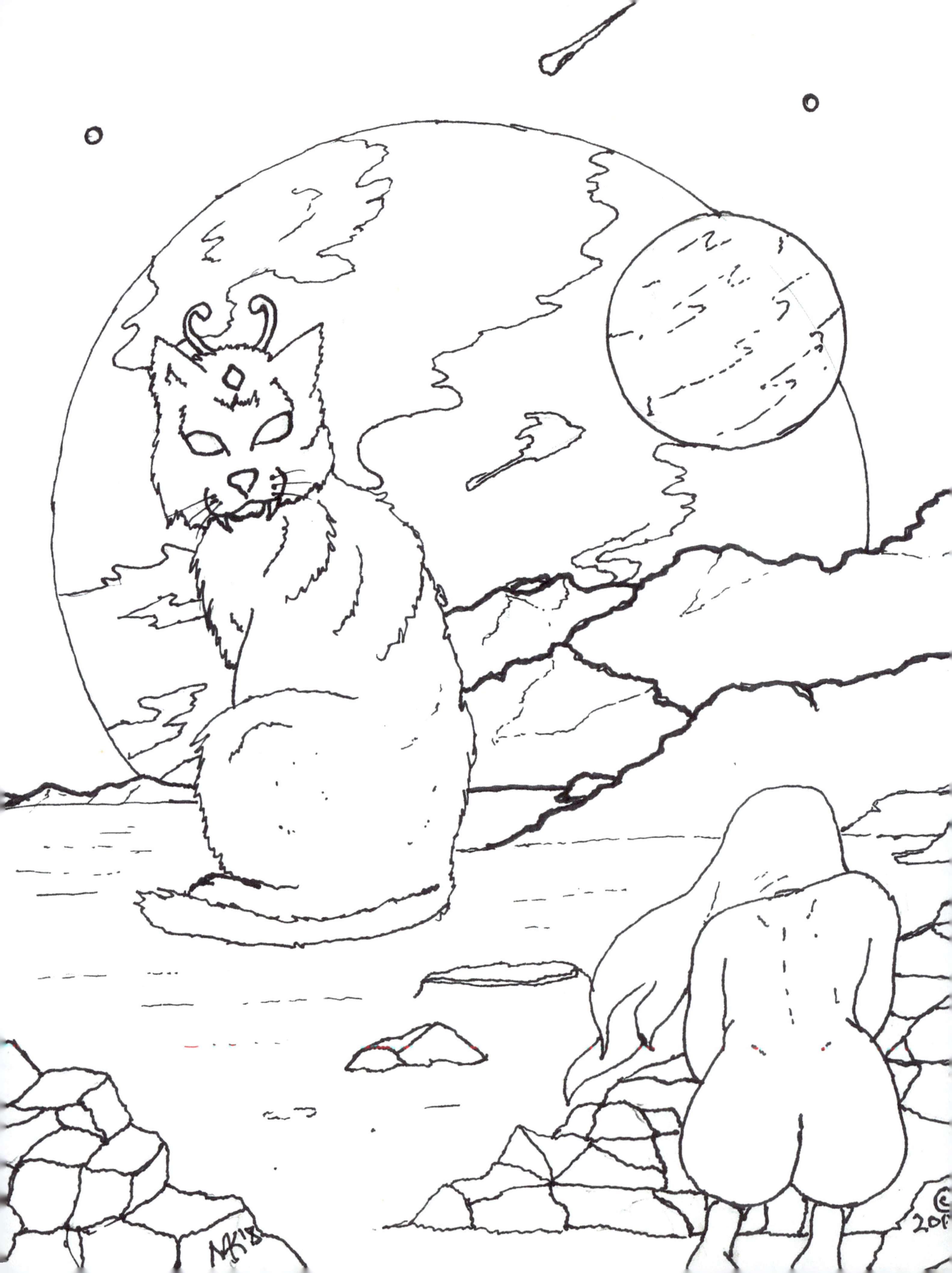

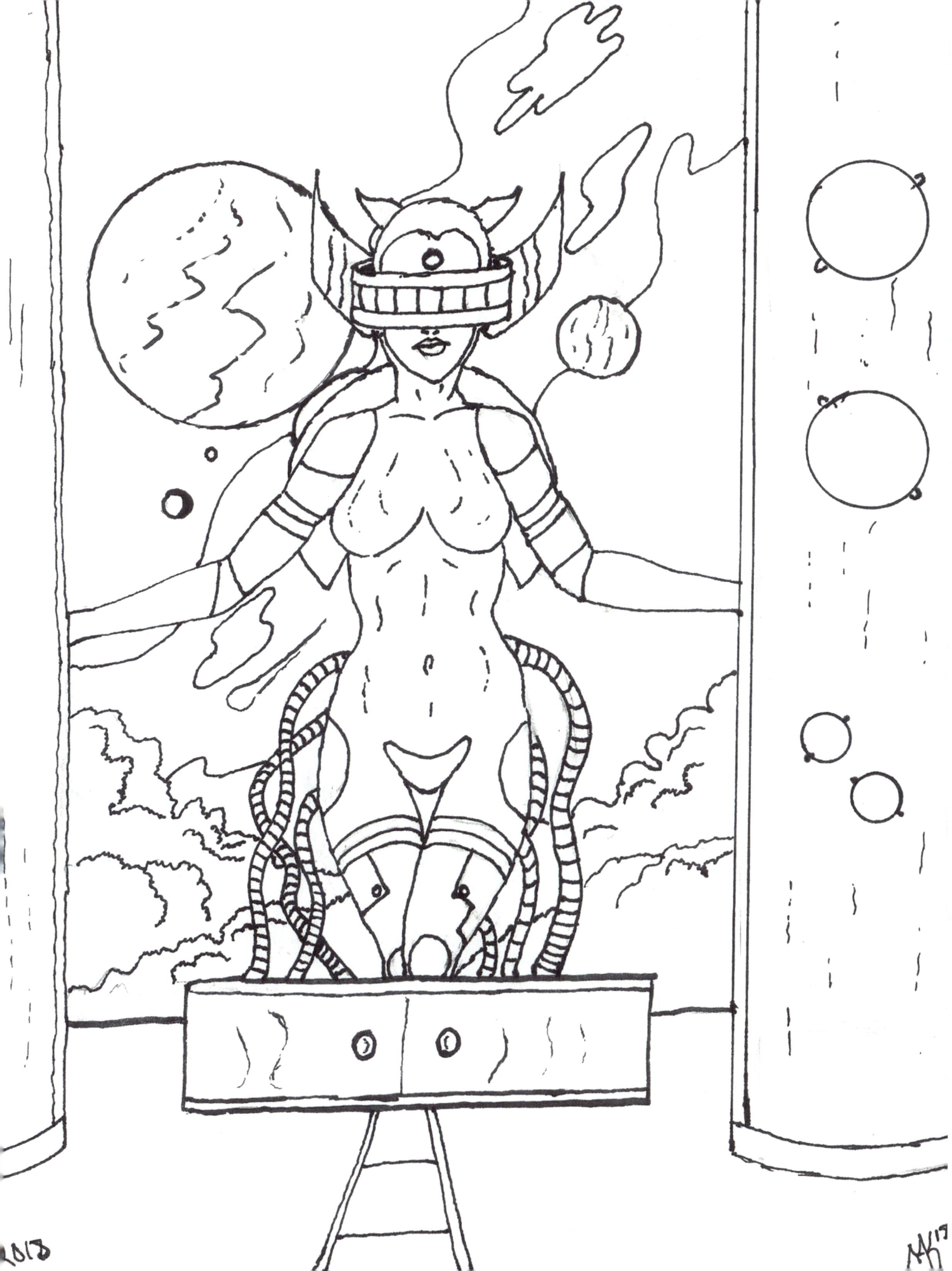

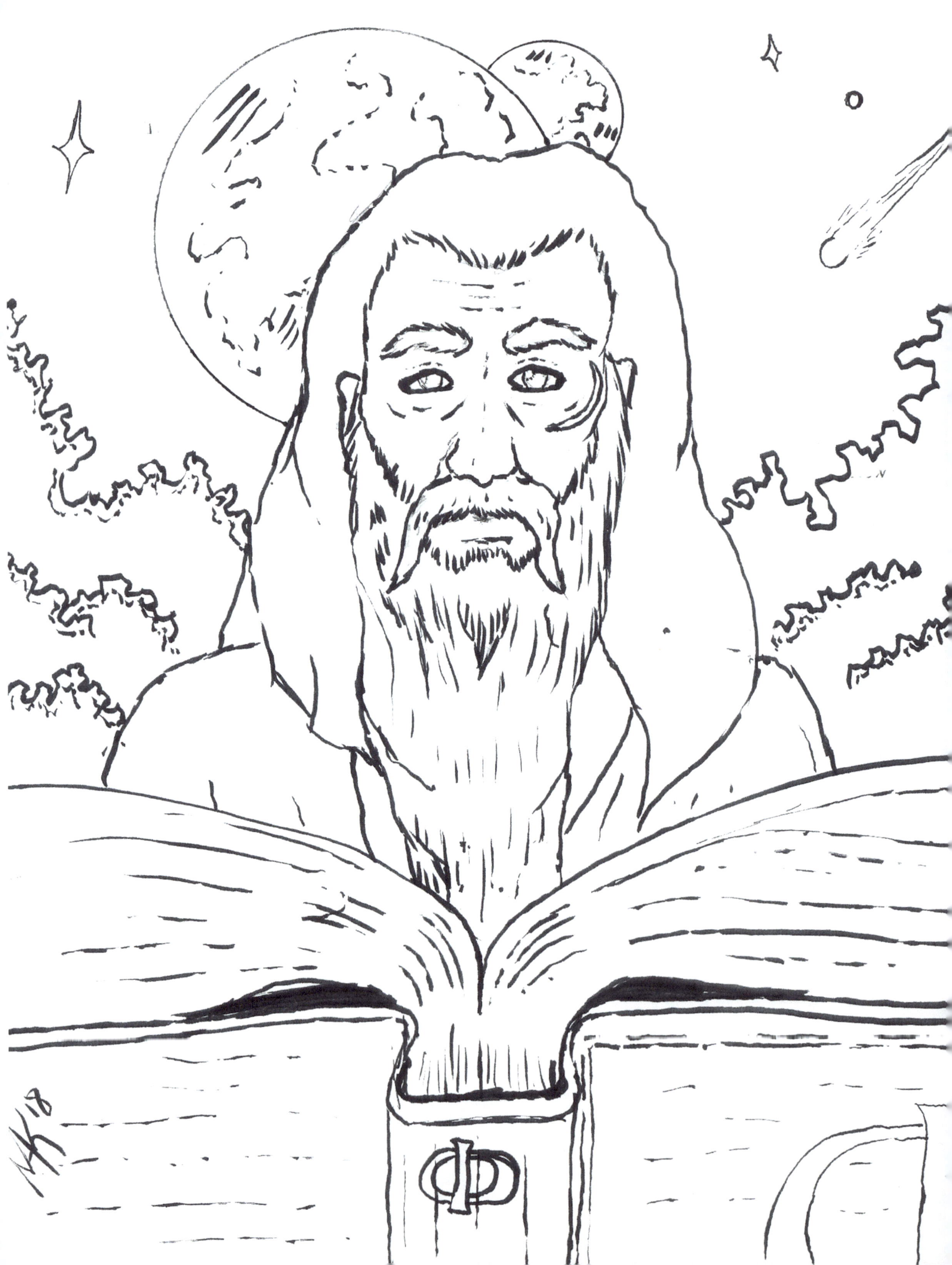

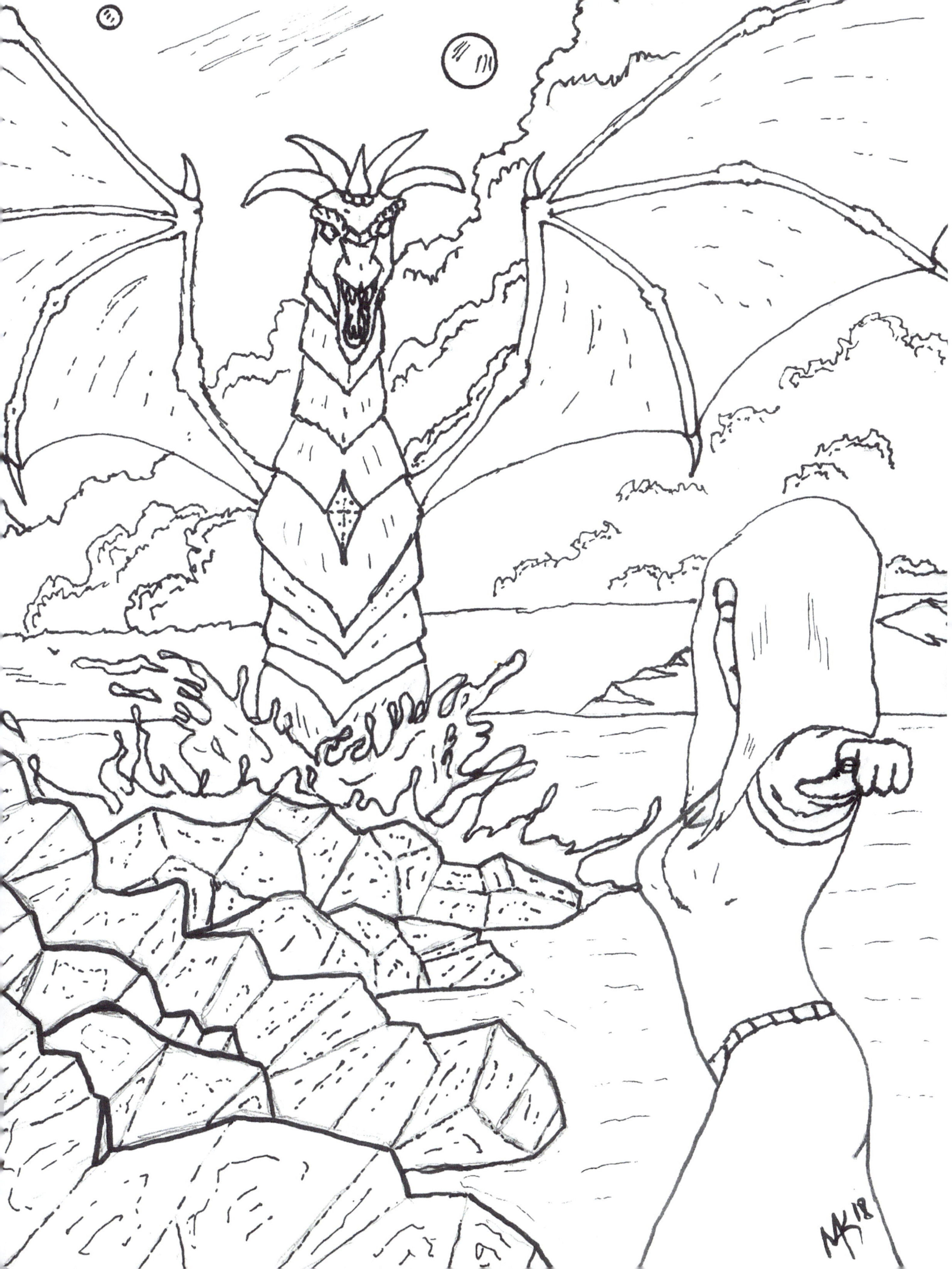

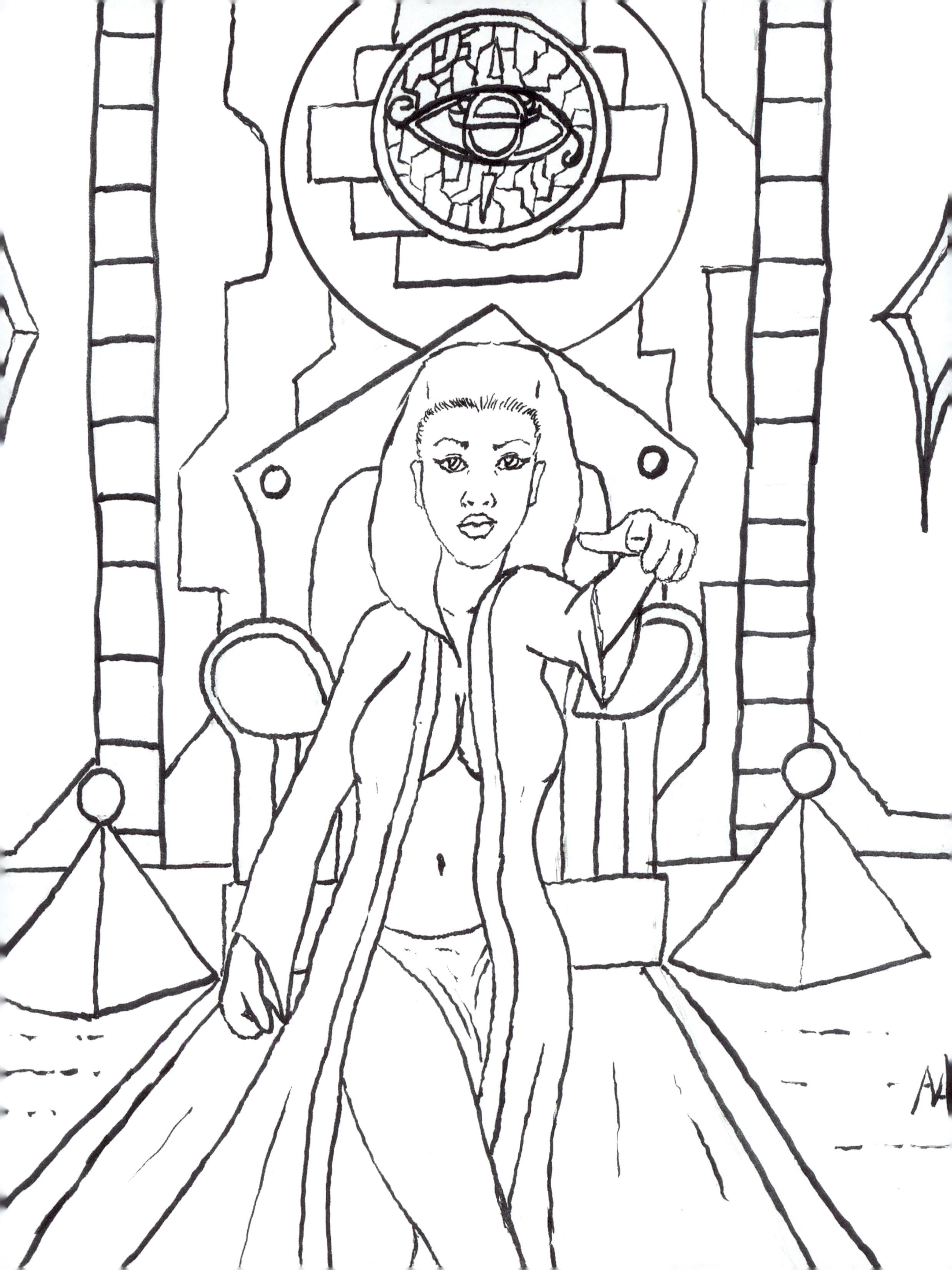

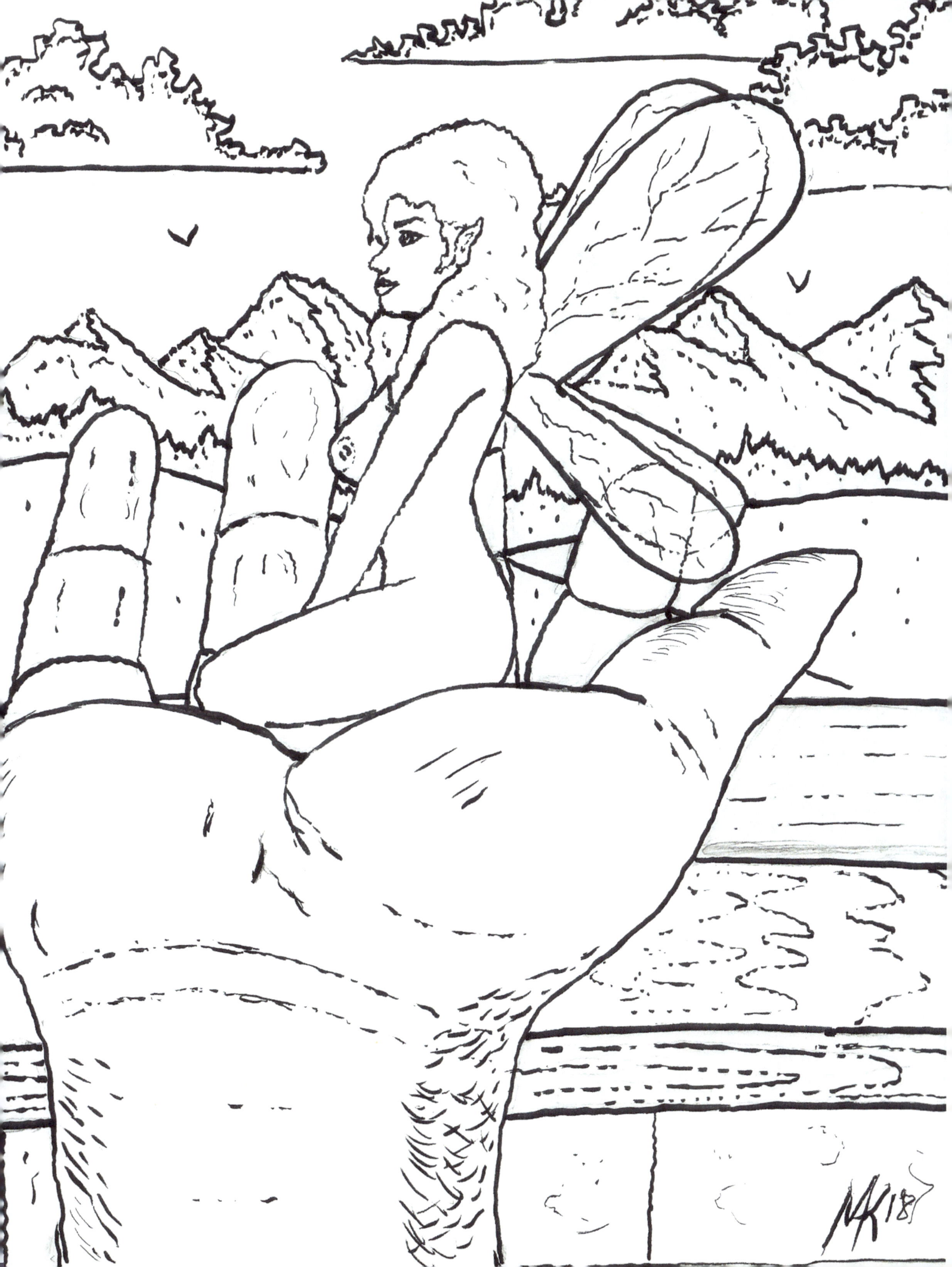

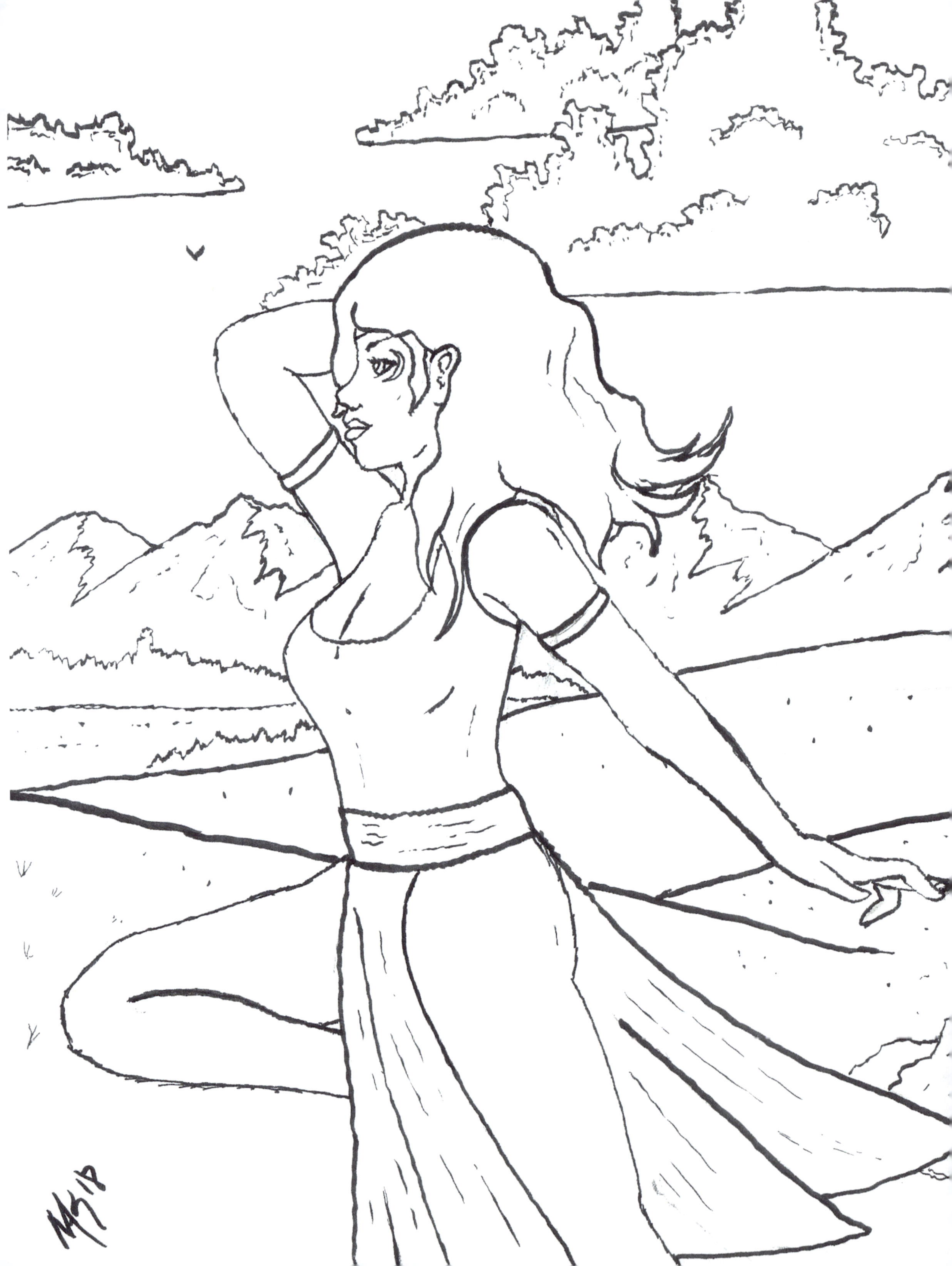

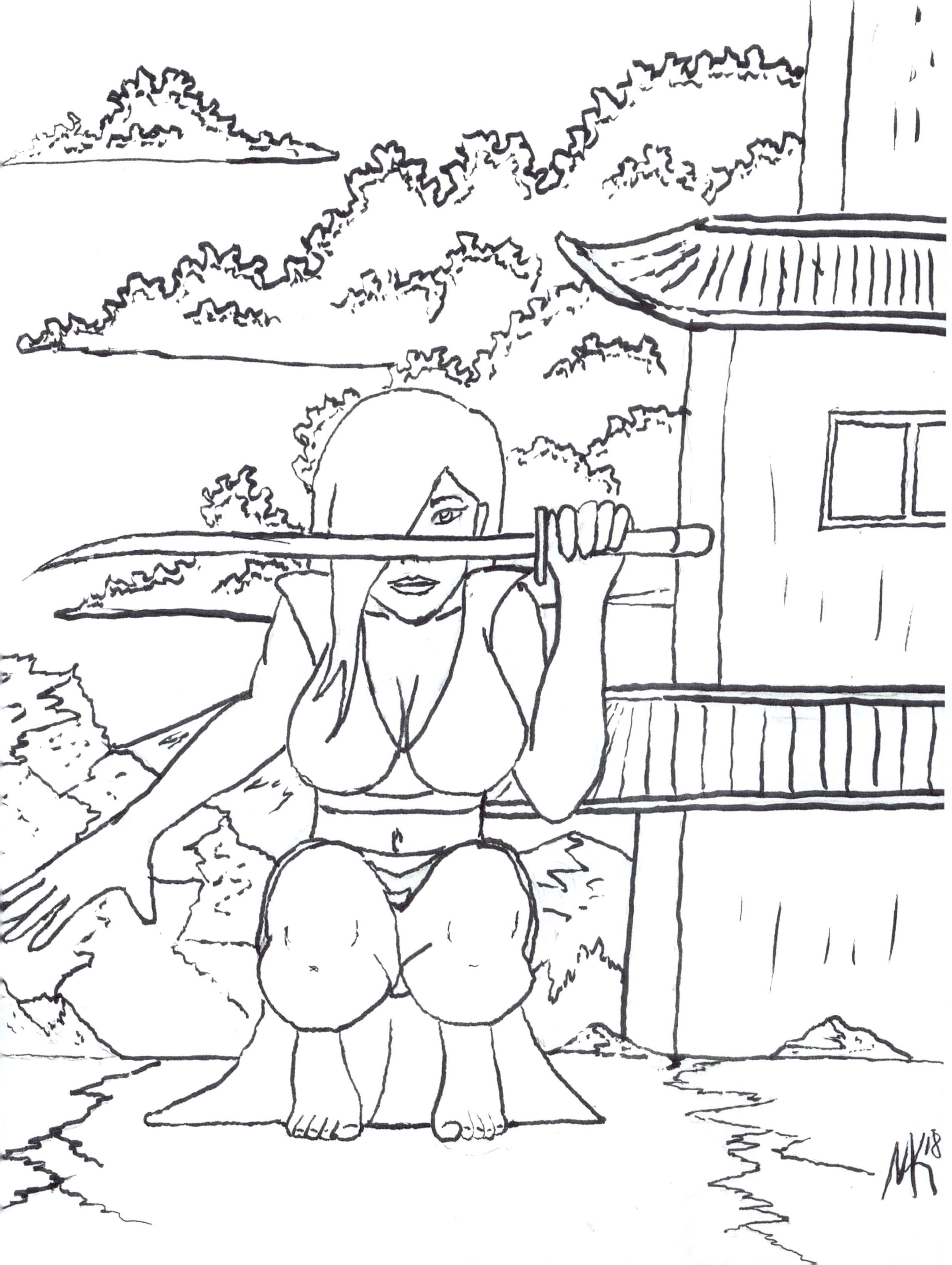

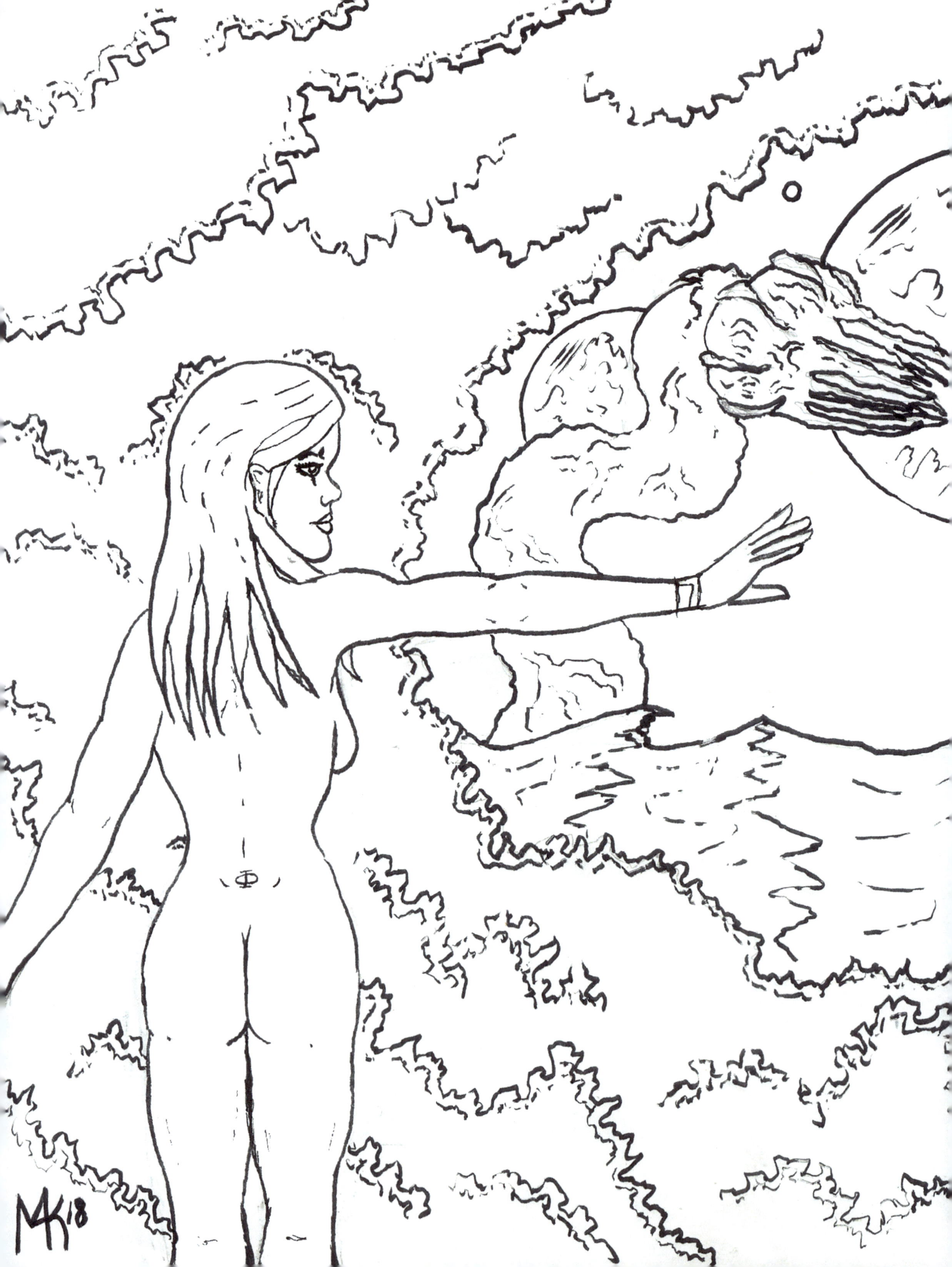

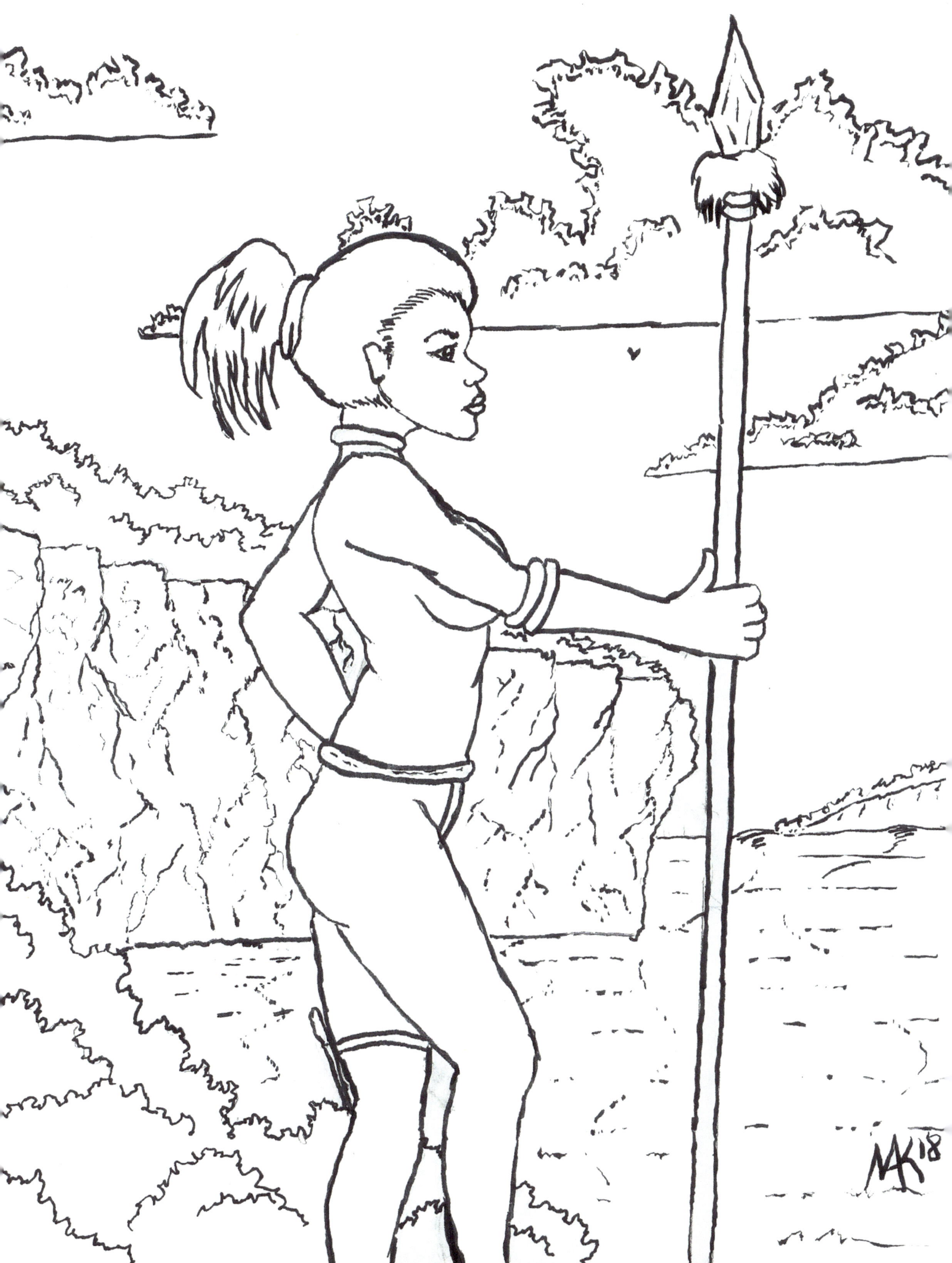

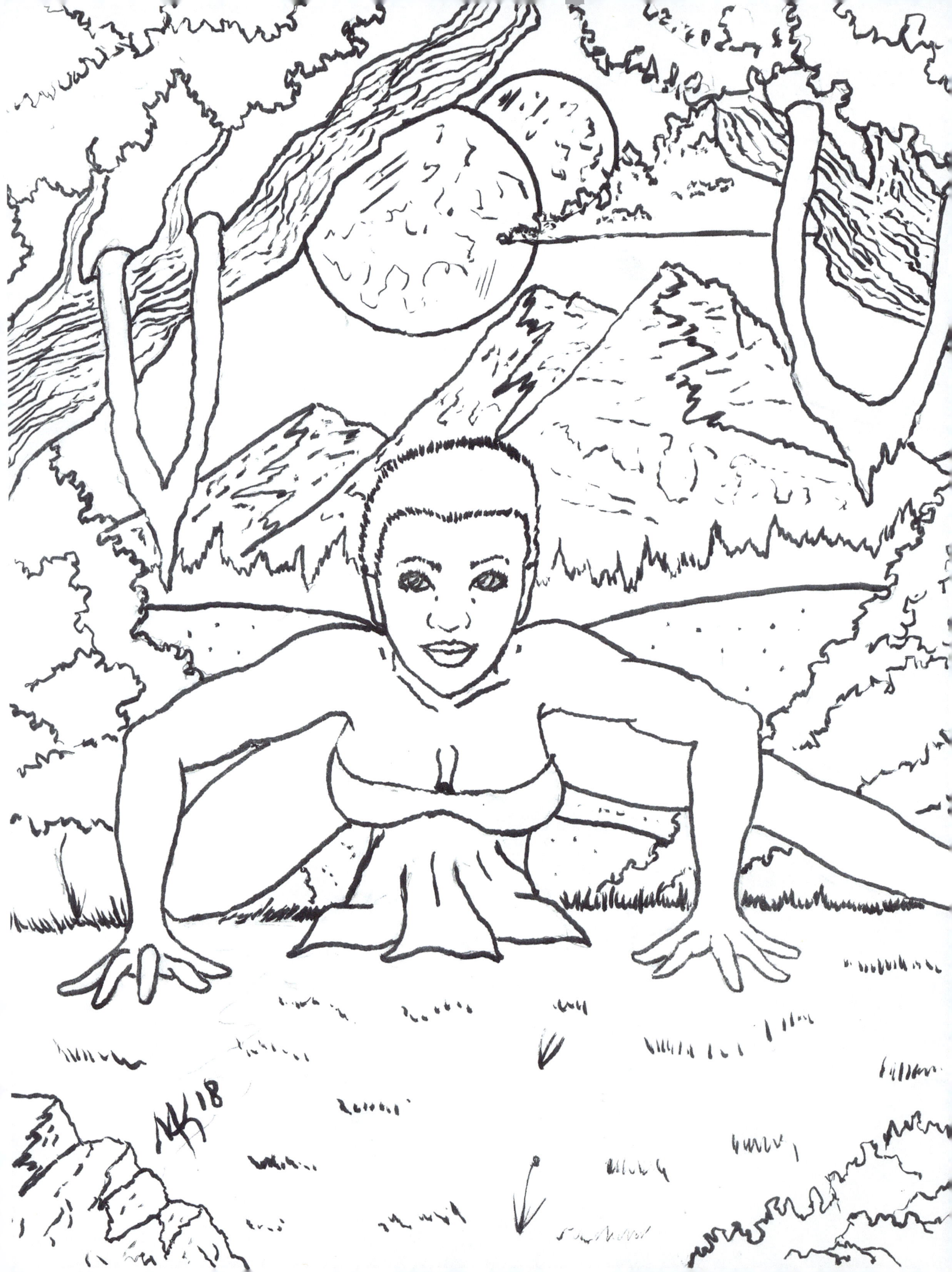

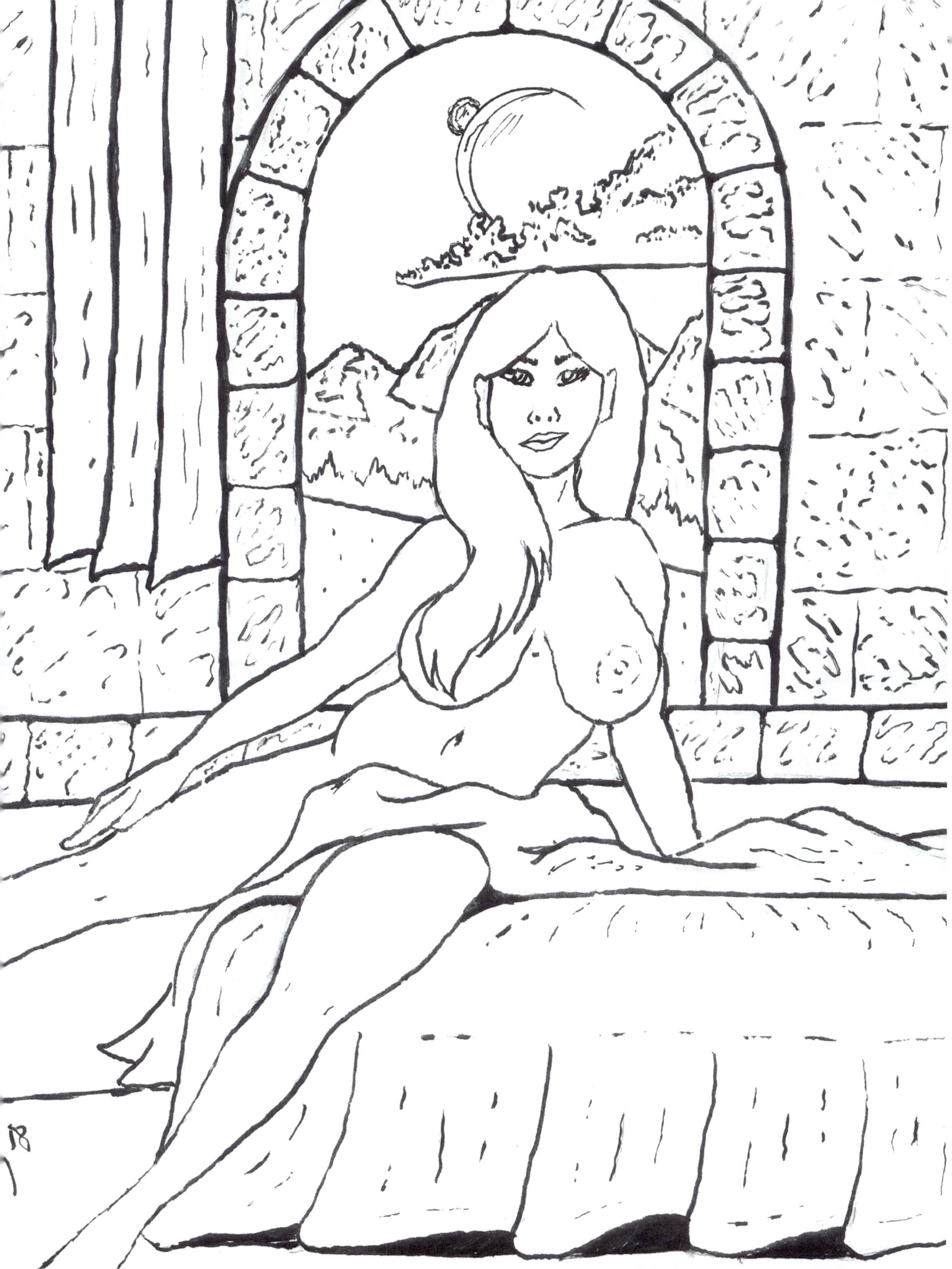

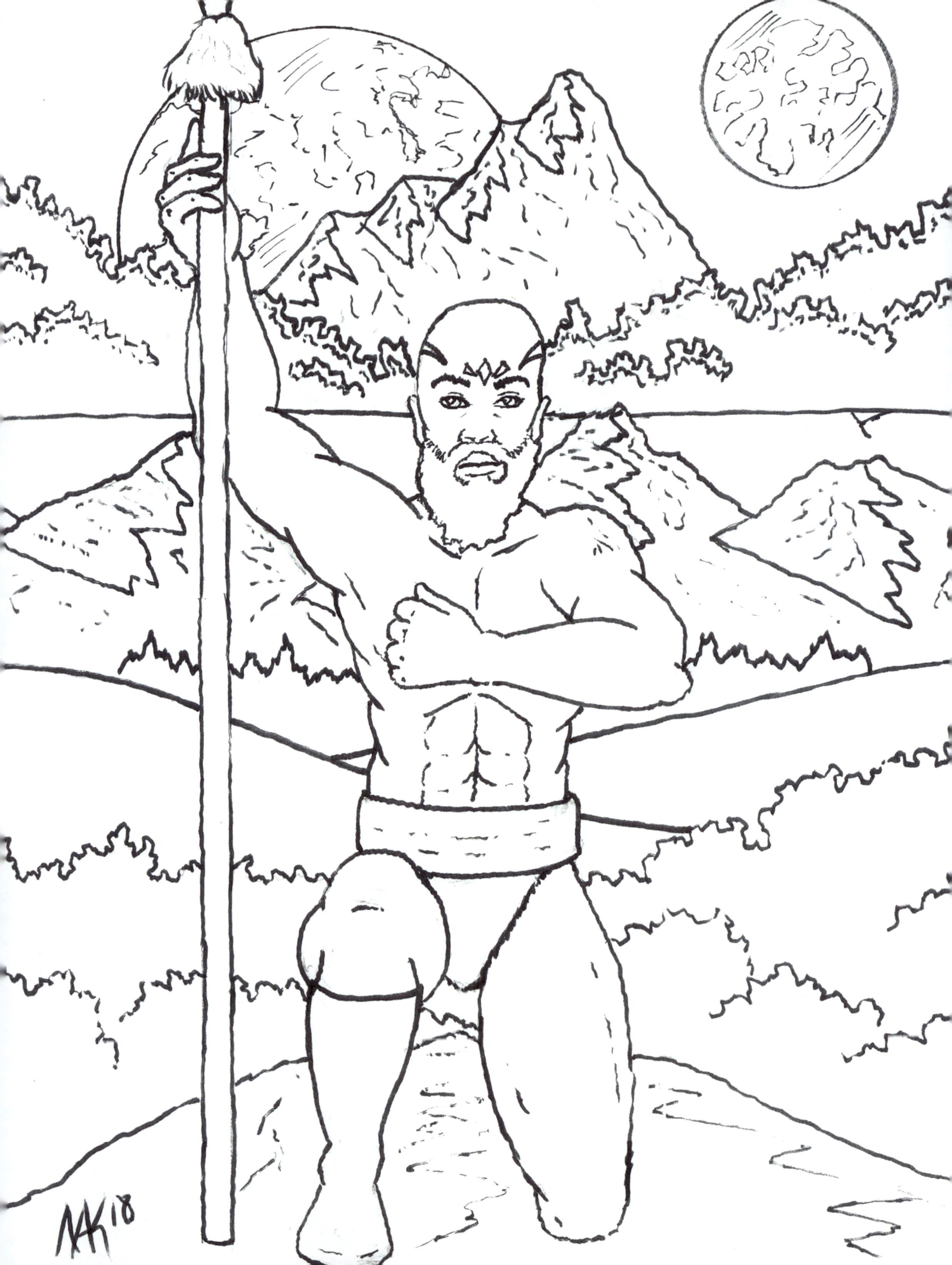

NAK'18

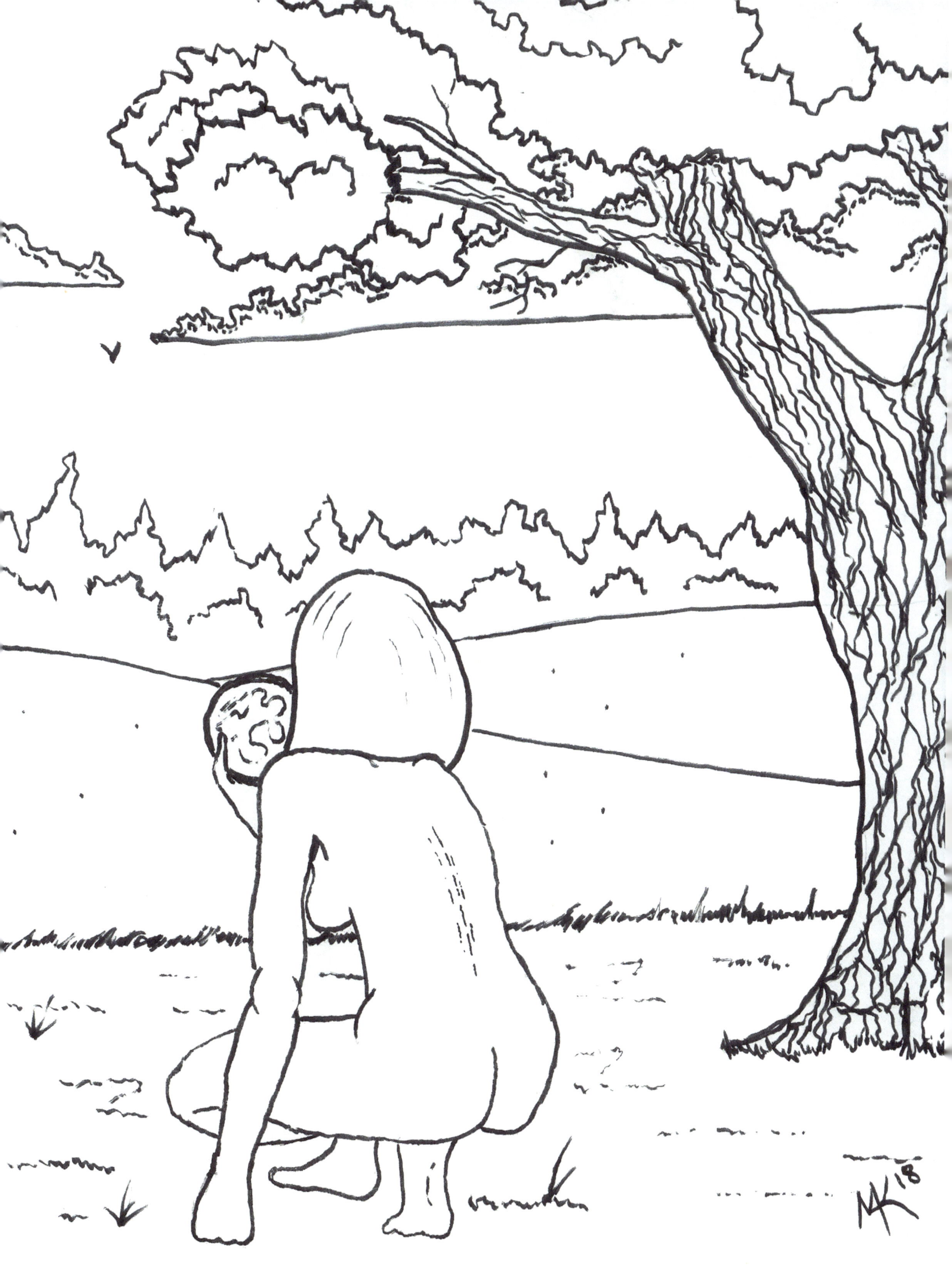

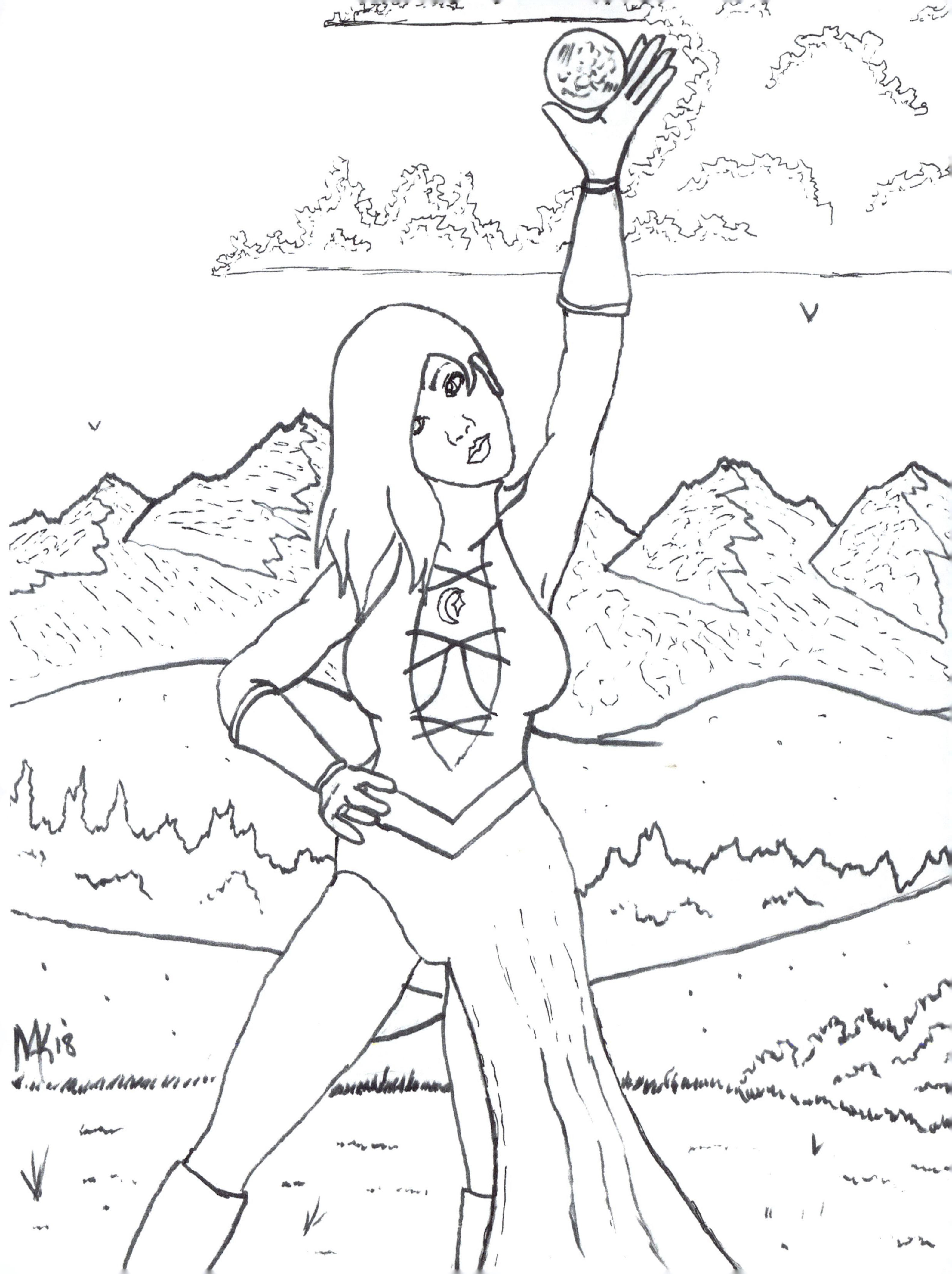

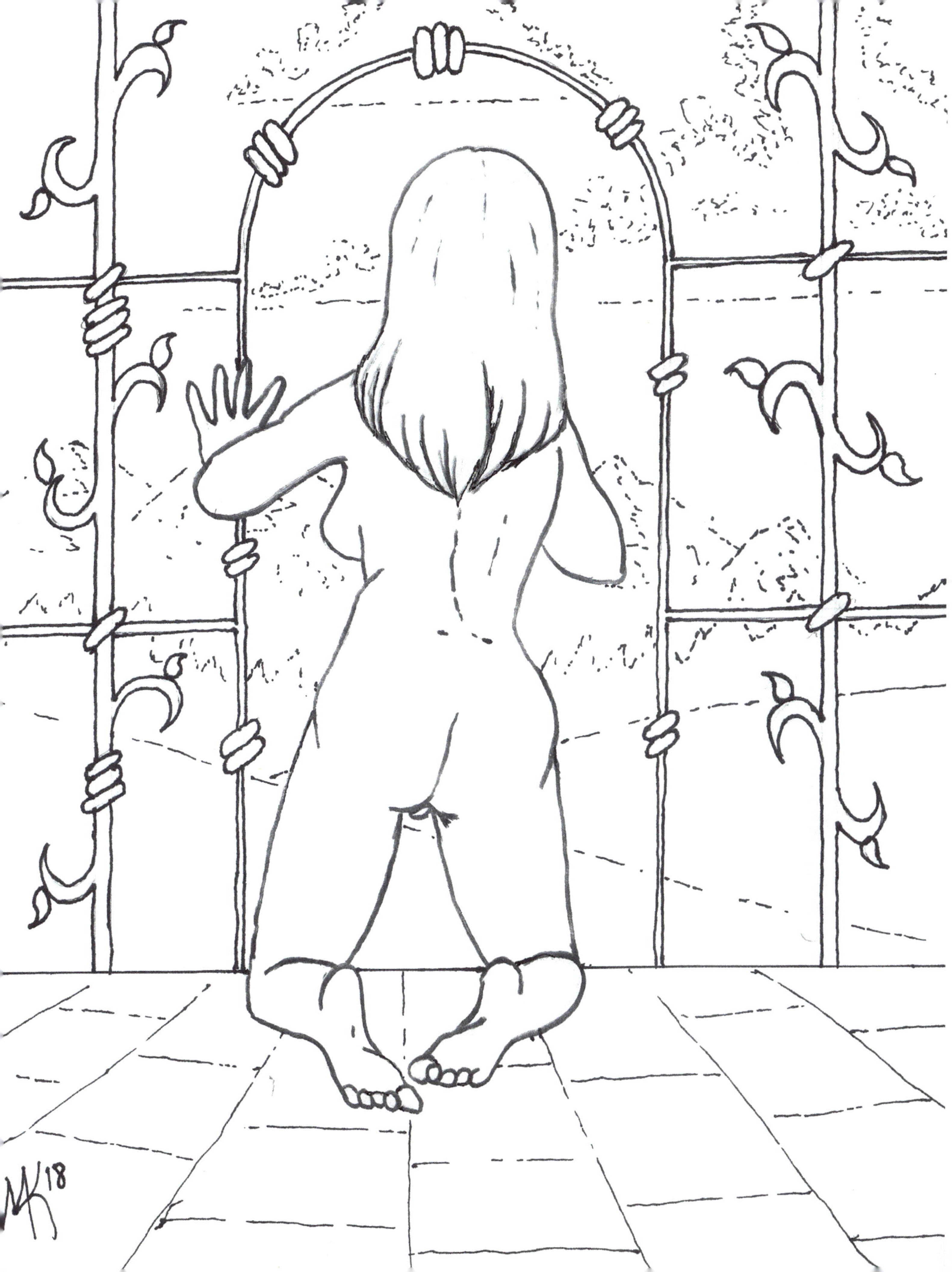

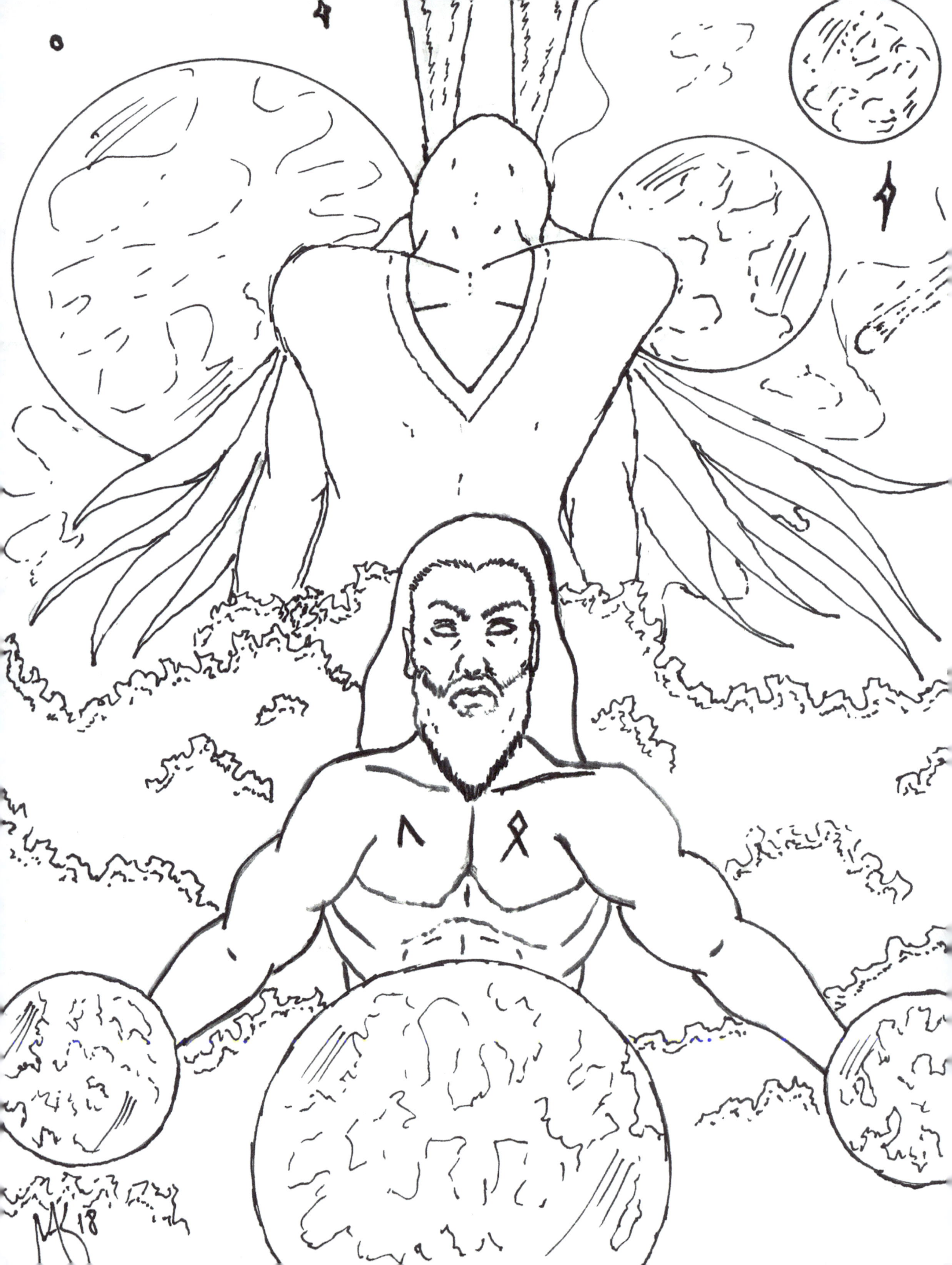

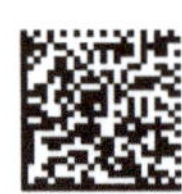

www.ingramcontent.com/pod-product-compliance
Lightning Source LLC
Chambersburg PA
CBHW042126030726
47599CB00002B/360